History and Hate:

The Dimensions of Anti-Semitism

History
and Hate
The Dimensions of
Anti-Semitism

edited by **David Berger**

THE JEWISH PUBLICATION SOCIETY
Philadelphia • New York • Jerusalem   *5747 • 1986*

Library of Congress Cataloging in Publication Data
History and hate.

   Includes index.
   1. Antisemitism—History.   I. Berger, David,
1943–
DS145.H56   1986   305.8'924   86–2995
ISBN 0–8276–0267–7

Designed by Adrianne Onderdonk Dudden

To Pearl,

Miriam, Yitzhak, and Gedalyah

Contents

Preface

Anti-Semitism has been the subject of many fine works, ranging from multi-volume surveys, like Leon Poliakov's *History of Anti-Semitism,* through book-length studies of entire periods, like Jacob Katz's *From Prejudice to Destruction: Anti-Semitism 1700–1933,* to a host of scholarly books and articles examining points of detail. Nevertheless, this volume presents the issues in a manner that should provide both fresh insights and useful synthesis for student, scholar, and general reader; unlike its recent predecessors, it covers the entire sweep of the history of anti-Semitism through sharply focused analyses of each major era by first-rate scholars expert in the specific period they discuss.

This book emerged from a conference sponsored by The Anti-Defamation League of B'nai B'rith and by The Joseph and Ceil Mazer Institute for Research and Advanced Studies in Judaica of the Center for Jewish Studies, City University of New York. It is a special pleasure to thank Theodore Freedman of ADL for his central role in coordinating the conference and Yael Zerubavel of the Center for Jewish Studies for her assistance in ensuring its success.

David Berger

Brooklyn College and the Graduate Center,
City University of New York

History and Hate:

The Dimensions of Anti-Semitism

Anti-Semitism:
An Overview

David Berger

We shall never fully understand anti-Semitism. Deep-rooted, complex, endlessly persistent, constantly changing yet remaining the same, it is a phenomenon that stands at the intersection of history, sociology, economics, political science, religion, and psychology. But it is often the most elusive phenomena that are the most intriguing, and here fascination and profound historical significance merge to make this subject a central challenge to Jewish historians.

Despite its nineteenth-century context and its often inappropriate racial implications, the term *anti-Semitism* has become so deeply entrenched that resistance to its use is probably futile. The impropriety of the term, however, makes it all the more important to clarify as fully as possible the range of meanings that can legitimately be assigned to it. Essentially, anti-Semitism means either of the following: (1) hostility toward Jews as a group which results from no legitimate cause or greatly exceeds any reasonable, ethical response to genuine provocation; or (2) a pejorative perception of Jewish physical or moral traits which is either utterly groundless or a result of irrational generalization and exaggeration.

These definitions can place an atypical and sometimes unwelcome burden on historians, who must consequently make ethical judgments a central part of historical analysis. When is a cause legitimate or a provocation genuine? At what point does a generalization become irrational or a response exceedingly unethical? Most anti-Semites have unfortunately made such evaluations very simple, but, as Shaye Cohen indicates in his contribution to this volume, these questions become particularly acute when one deals with anti-Semitism in antiquity.

The earliest references to Jews in the Hellenistic world are positive ones, and the attraction of Judaism for many pagans continued well into the Christian era. When anti-Jewish sentiment arises, it can usually be explained by causative factors of a straightforward sort: Jewish refusal to worship local gods, missionizing, revolutionary activity, dietary separatism, and marital exclusivity. Some of these, at least, can be perceived as "legitimate" grievances, although a number of the pagan reactions so violate the requirements of proportionality that they cross the threshold into anti-Semitism. In any event, we have no reason to believe that we are dealing in this case with a phenomenon that resists ordinary historical explanation. If one were to insist on defining anti-Semitism as a pathology, then its existence in the ancient world has yet to be demonstrated.

As pagan antiquity gives way to the Christian Middle Ages, we confront the first crucial transition in the history of anti-Semitism. Much has been written about the question of continuity and disjunction at this point: Did Christianity, for all its original contributions to the theory of Jew-hatred, essentially continue a pre-existing strand in classical thought and society, or did it create virtually *de novo* a virulent strain that bears but a superficial resemblance to the anti-Semitism of old? Despite the sharpness of the formulation, the alternatives posed in this question are not, in fact, mutually exclusive. It would violate common sense to deny that classical anti-Semitism provided fertile soil for the growth of the medieval variety, and despite the demise of the ancient gods and the waning of Jewish missionizing and rebelliousness, some of the older grievances retained their force.

Nevertheless, if ancient paganism had been replaced by a religion or ideology without an internal anti-Jewish dynamic, it is likely that the anti-Semitism of the classical world would have gradually faded. Instead, it was reinforced. The old, pedestrian causes of anti-Jewish animus were replaced by a new, powerful myth of extraordinary force and vitality.

Medieval Christian theology expresses a profound love-hate relationship with Judaism. Of all religions in the world, only Judaism may be tolerated under the cross, for Jews serve as unwilling, unwitting witnesses of Christian truth. This testimony arises from Jewish authentication of the Hebrew Scriptures, which in turn authenticate Christianity, but it also arises from Jewish suffering, whose severity and duration can be explained only as divine retribution for the sin of the crucifixion. Hence, the same theology that accorded Jews a unique toleration required them to undergo unique persecution.

In the early Middle Ages, it was the tolerant element in this position that predominated. With the great exception of seventh-century Visigothic Spain, persecution of Jews in pre-Crusade Europe was sporadic and desultory; the regions north and west of Italy had no indigenous anti-Semitic tradition, and Christianity had not yet struck deep enough roots in mass psychology to generate the emotional force necessary for the wreaking of vengeance on the agents of the crucifixion. Early medieval Europeans worshipped Jesus, but it is not clear that they loved him enough.

This is not to say that the course of medieval anti-Semitism is to be charted by reference to religious developments alone, although religion is almost surely the crucial guide. The deterioration of Jewish security in the high Middle Ages and beyond corresponds to transformations in economic, political, and intellectual history as well; indeed, the fact that a variety of changes that may well have affected anti-Semitism unfolded in rough synchronism makes it difficult to untangle the causal skeins but at the same time provides a richer and more satisfying explanatory network.

Christian piety widened and deepened, and the spectacular outbreaks of Jew-hatred during the Crusades were surely nourished by pietistic excess. As mercantile and administrative experience spread through an increasingly literate and urbanized Christian bourgeoisie, the economic need for Jews declined precipitously; it is no accident that in the later Middle Ages Jews were welcome primarily in less-developed regions like thirteenth-century Spain and, even later, Bohemia, Austria, and Poland. To make matters worse, the remaining economic activity in which Jews came to be concentrated was a natural spawning-ground for intense hostility: Moneylending may be a necessity, but it does not generate affection. In the political sphere, the high Middle Ages saw the beginnings of a sense of national unity at least in France and England; although this fell short of genuine nationalism in the modern sense, it sharpened the perception of the Jew as the quintessential alien. Finally, despite the centrifugal effects of individual nationalisms, the concept of a monochromatic European Christendom also grew, and with it came heightened intolerance toward any form of deviation.

At a time of growing friction with ordinary Christians, Jews were obliged to look for protection to kings and churchmen. Since riots against Jews violated the law and undermined public order, appeals for royal protection were sometimes heeded. Of equal importance, kings had begun to look upon Jewish holdings—and even upon the Jews themselves—as property of the royal treasury, with the ironic result that protection might well be forthcoming to safeguard the financial interests of the king. Alternatively, however, the process of fiscal exploitation and confiscation could just as easily culminate in outright expulsion.

Appeals to the clergy produced similarly mixed results. The theoretical position of canon law concerning Jewish toleration was no longer a self-evident assumption governing the status of the Jews in a relatively tolerant society; it required constant reaffirmation in a Europe where it had frequently become not only the last line of Jewish defense but also the first. It was for this reason alone that St. Bernard of Clairvaux, who had little affection for Jews, intervened to save Jewish lives during the second Crusade, and it is symptomatic of the new circumstances that a Jewish chronicler considers it noteworthy that he took no money for this intervention. Moreover, fissures were developing in the theory of toleration itself. The Talmud was investigated in Paris and burned at the behest of the Church; on occasion, even expulsions came to be regarded as not altogether inconsistent with a policy of toleration, since they fell short of the shedding of blood. Only the innate conservatism characteristic of any system of religious law protected the core of the position from concerted attack, so that Jews could continue to hope—ever more wistfully—for the protection of an increasingly hostile Church.

As the Middle Ages drew to a close, a new specter began haunting the Jews of Europe—the specter of demonology. The growing importance of the devil and his minions in late medieval Europe far transcends the Jewish question. Nevertheless, plague, war, and depression created an atmosphere, especially in northern lands, in which the explanation for terror and tragedy was sought in the alliance between the Jewish adversary and the Adversary himself. Jews, it was said, perpetrated ritual murder, consuming the blood—and sometimes the hearts—of their victims; Jews poisoned wells and Jewish doctors poisoned patients; consecrated hosts were stolen, pierced, and beaten; the Jewish stench and other unique illnesses and deformities underscored the alienness and dubious humanity of the lecherous vicars of Satan. It was not only the folk imagination that could depict a Jewish woman who gives birth to swine; fifteenth-century intellectuals from Spain to Bohemia could speak of Jews as the offspring of a liaison between Adam and demons or as the product not of the patriarchs' seed but of their excrement. The vulgar fulminations in the late works of Luther did not arise *ex nihilo*.

The perception of Jews as forces of darkness in the most fearsome and tangible sense was especially conducive to the expulsions and brutalities that mark late medieval Jewish history, but the belief that Jewish alienness transcends religious differences was important in another context as well. When Jews converted to Christianity singly or in tiny groups, it was relatively easy to accept them unreservedly with the full measure of Christian love. In fourteenth- and fifteenth-century Spain, however, Christians had to deal with the new phenomenon of mass conversion. This, of course, created economic tensions that are not generated by individual conversions, but it must also have produced a psychological dilemma: It is extraordinarily difficult for a society to transform its attitude toward an entire group virtually overnight. There were, it is true, plausible arguments that the religious sincerity of these new Christians left something to be desired; nevertheless, the reluctance to accord them a full welcome into the Christian fold went beyond such considerations. Despite the absence of a prominent demonic motif, the Marranos faced at least an embryonic manifestation of racial anti-Semitism, which served as a refuge for a hostile impulse that could no longer point to palpable distinctions.

This figure of the hated new Christian adumbrates the hated acculturated Jew of later centuries and points the way toward the crucial transition to modern times. Like the passing of pagan antiquity and the emergence of Christian dominance, the waning of the Middle Ages was marked by fundamental ideological change. By the eighteenth century, Christianity began to lose its hold on important elements of the intellectual elite, and once again there seemed to be potential for the eradication or radical weakening of anti-Semitism. The transition of the eighteenth century, however, was far more complex than that of the fourth.

First of all, the old ideology did not disappear. There were areas of Europe, most notably in the east, where the commitment to traditional forms of Christianity retained its full force into the nineteenth century and beyond. Even in the west, large sectors of the early modern population remained immune to the impact of Enlightenment and secularization, so that old-style hostility to Jews could continue to flourish. A second complicating factor is

David Berger

that this time there are periods and places in which anti-Semitism *did* wane, and analysis of its modern manifestations must balance explanations for persistence against reasons for decline. Finally, the stated reasons for modern Jew-hatred are more varied and mutable than their medieval equivalents. In the Middle Ages, whatever the role of economic and political factors, the religious basis for anti-Semitism was a constant throughout the period, forming a permanent foundation that served as both underlying reason and stated rationale. In the modern era, on the other hand, we are presented with a shifting, dizzying kaleidoscope of often contradictory explanations: The Jews are Rothschilds and paupers, capitalists and communists, nationalists and deracinated cosmopolitans, religious separatists and dangerous free thinkers, evil geniuses and the possessors of superficial, third-rate minds.

We must beware of easy psychological reductionism, which excuses the historian from a careful examination of the complexities of modern anti-Semitism. Nevertheless, this list of grievances against Jews suggests that by the modern period anti-Semitism had reached the level of a deeply rooted pathology. It is precisely because Jews were the only significant minority in medieval Christian Europe that the fear and hatred of the alien became fixed upon them; a fixation that develops over a millennium is not uprooted merely by the slow weakening of its major cause. Hence, the arguments proposed by modern anti-Semites—and by historians who try to understand them—reflect a complex interweaving of reason and rationalization, of genuine cause and shifting, often elusive excuse.

With the passing of Christian dominance, anti-Semitism in the modern West came to be associated with other ideological issues that in large measure replaced Christianity as the focus of European concerns. The first of these was nationalism. At first glance, the egalitarian spirit of the French Revolution appears utterly incompatible with the persistence of Jewish disabilities, and the emancipation of the Jews was, in fact, achieved. But the increasing power of the national state—and its increasing demands—provided ammunition for a new, exceptionally powerful argument against such emancipation. The eighteenth-century state demanded not only its residents' toil and sweat but also their hearts and souls: full loyalty, total identification, fervent patriotism. Moreover, the breakdown of the old regime's corporate structure required the citizen to engage in an unmediated relationship with the centralized state. Jews, it was said, failed these tests. In descent and behavior, in communal structure and emotional ties, Jews were an alien nation, a state within a state, no more deserving of citizenship than Frenchmen in Germany or Germans in France. Since the nature of the state had changed so much that retention of medieval status was hardly a realistic option, this analysis posed no small threat to Jewish security.

The only viable response, it seemed, was the denial of Jewish nationhood. So Jews denied it—and they denied it sincerely. There is at least faint irony in Jews' declaring that they are not a nation while anti-Semites vigorously affirm that they are, but the gradual spread of Jewish emancipation through much of nineteenth-century Europe awakened feelings of genuine, profound patriotism that led to the defining of Judaism in the narrowest confessional terms. Until late in the century, this sacrifice—which most western Jews considered no sacrifice at all—appeared to have achieved its goal. Barriers crumbled, discrimination eased, redemption-in-exile appeared at hand.

Nevertheless, like so many earlier, more traditional instances of messianic aspirations, this one too was doomed to disappointment. The more Jews behaved like Christians, the stranger it seemed that they would not become Christians, and even in a more secularized age, conversion remained the symbol and *sine qua non* of full entry into Gentile society. On occasion, an act of acculturation and rapprochement would paradoxically lead to increased tensions. Reform Judaism, for example, de-emphasized ritual while stressing ethics, much as liberal Protestantism had elevated ethics and downgraded dogma. However, in the absence of conversion of Reform Jews, this agreement on content led to an acrimonious dispute over which religion had the legitimate claim to the ethical message preached by both sides, and Christian denigration of Jewish ethics became a theme that bordered on anti-Semitism. In a broader context, even Christian supporters of Jewish emancipation had generally expected it to bring about the gradual disappearance of the Jews, and the failure of most Jews to cooperate left a sense of disquiet and frustration. Additionally, as Todd Endelman stresses in this volume, the resurgence of anti-Semitism in the late nineteenth century was part of a general rebellion against the liberalism and modernity that were responsible for emancipating the Jews.

In a world of acculturated Jews, how was this new anti-Semitism to be expressed? Many of the anti-Semitic political parties pressed economic and religious grievances of a quite traditional sort, but there were difficulties in arguing that the Jews of France and Germany were so different from Christians that they posed a genuine, alien threat. There was, however, a more promising approach—explosive, sinister, closer to the psychic wellsprings of popular anti-Semitism, and immune to the argument that Jews were, after all, "improving." Racial categories were prominent and universal in nineteenth-century European thought; to some degree, they had been used against Jews from the earliest days of emancipation, and Jews themselves evinced no hesitation in assigning special characteristics—sometimes even physical ones—to the Jewish "race." For anti-Semites—and it is in this context that the term was coined—the "polluted" racial character of the Jews served, as it had in the Marrano period, as a basis for hating people whose distinctiveness could not readily be discerned. The unacculturated Jew was a visible enemy; the acculturated one—despite caricatures of Jewish physical traits—was insidious, camouflaged, coiled to strike at European society from within. Jewish acculturation was no longer a promise; it was a threat.

It is no accident that the worst manifestation of Jew-hatred in history was built upon this foundation. Nazi anti-Semitism

achieved such virulent, unrestrained consequences precisely because it stripped away the semi-civilized rationales that had been
given in the past for persecuting Jews and liberated the deepest
psychic impulses that had been partly nurtured but partly sup-
pressed by those rationales. Although the Nazis used the standard
political, economic, and sometimes even religious arguments for
persecution, their central message was that Jews were alien,
demonic creatures, subhuman and superhuman at the same time,
who threatened "Aryans" with racial corruption and with profound, almost inexpressible terror. Such feelings were probably a
part of the anti-Semitic psyche for centuries, and I have already
argued that the deeply rooted fear and hatred of the alien had
become fixed upon the Jews; nevertheless, these feelings had not
been given free reign. The persecution of political enemies, economic exploiters, and religious deviants must still be governed by
a modicum of civilized restraint; although this restraint must have
seemed invisible to the victims of the Crusades, it reappears,
however dimly, when seen through the prism of the Holocaust.
On the other hand, malevolent demons, racial aliens, and malig-
nant vermin can be extirpated with single-minded, ruthless
ferocity.*

One of the most significant reactions to the new anti-
Semitism was the rise of Jewish nationalism. To many observers
—including many Jews—this was an abrogation of the original,
unwritten contract granting Jews emancipation; nevertheless,
the Zionist movement did not play a major role in the upsurge of
European anti-Semitism in the decades before the Holocaust. Its
impact on anti-Semitism came in different, quite unexpected
ways: in the grafting of western Jew-hatred onto the traditional
patterns of discrimination in the Muslim world, and in providing
a new outlet and a new camouflage for the anti-Semitic impulse.

*Much of the language in this paragraph is borrowed from my "Jewish-
Christian Relations: A Jewish Perspective," *Journal of Ecumenical Studies* 20
(1983): 23.

David Berger

Pre-modern Jews had flourished and suffered under Islam, but anti-Jewish sentiment rarely reached the heights that it attained in the Christian world. This was partly because Jews were never the only minority in the Muslim orbit, but it was also because Judaism did not play the crucial role in Islam that it did in Christianity. The frequent Christian obsession with Jews was nourished in large measure by resentment toward a parent with whom intimate contact could not be avoided; Islam's relationship with Judaism lacked that intimacy and hence failed to generate the sort of tensions that explode into violence. Persecutions of Jews in the Muslim world should not be minimized, but they are not of the same order of magnitude as anti-Jewish outbreaks in the Christian West.

However persuasive the claim of the Jewish people may be to its ancestral homeland, the failure of Arabs to embrace the Zionist immigrants was hardly unexpected and is not in itself grounds for a charge of anti-Semitism. But offended nationalist sentiments and old-style denigration of Jews combined to make the Arab world receptive to anti-Semitic propaganda ranging from *Mein Kampf* to *The Protocols of the Elders of Zion*. (The assertion that Arabs, as Semites, cannot be anti-Semitic is, of course, an overliteral and usually disingenuous argument.) Moreover, extreme forms of anti-Zionism outside the Arab world serve as a vehicle for anti-Semitic sentiments that are no longer respectable in their unalloyed, naked form. Here again there are genuine problems of definition, but "anti-Zionist" literature in the Soviet Union and the widespread application to Israel of an egregious double standard make it difficult to deny that anti-Zionism and anti-Semitism are not infrequently synonymous. The positions of the emancipation period have been reversed: Jews now lay claim to a nationhood that their enemies deny.

Anti-Semitism is no longer an acknowledged pillar of western thought and society. The distinguished medievalist R. W. Southern, in evaluating the normalcy or eccentricity of a major medieval churchman, correctly classified his "deep hostility to-ward the Jews" among the arguments for normalcy; had the subject of his evaluation been a contemporary western figure, such a classification would have been more than dubious. Despite the unspeakable agonies of twentieth-century European Jewry, anti-Semitism has not been wholly intractable.

At the same time, the nineteenth-century mixture of hope and expectation that Jew-hatred would fade away has proved to be a fantasy, and few indeed continue to indulge such dreams—surely not the Jew at a recent conference who confided his fears of the aftermath of nuclear war. He does not fear radiation, or climatic change, or wounds crying vainly for treatment; he worries instead that the war will be blamed on Einstein, Oppenheimer, and Teller.

Macabre Jewish humor, no doubt, or simple paranoia.

And yet . . .

Anti-Semitism in the Ancient World

Louis H. Feldman

"Almost every note in the cacophony of medieval and modern anti-Semitism was sounded by the chorus of ancient writers."[1] This observation is perfectly valid, but the phenomena that underlie it must be examined with meticulous care if we are to avoid hasty and exaggerated conclusions about the scope and intensity of classical anti-Semitism. First, the literary material itself is not unrelievedly hostile, and positive statements about Jews and Judaism must not be ignored. In addition, discussions of this subject often rest upon the assumption that the remarks of ancient intellectuals faithfully reflect societal attitudes in general. Thus a recent analyst declares that "a survey of the comments about Jews in the Hellenistic-Roman literature shows that they were almost universally disliked, or at least viewed with an amused contempt."[2] In fact, a separate analysis of the positions of government, the masses, and the intellectual elite will reveal a far more nuanced picture ranging from admiration to hostility to a toleration born of *Realpolitik*. Ancient anti-Semitism was significant and widespread, but it was part of a varied and complex reality.[3]

Governmental Anti-Semitism

Has anti-Semitism been universally prevalent? Probably not—
and in the case of government policy, surely not. After the biblical
Pharaoh (and one may question whether we should term his
policy "anti-Semitic" in view of the Egyptian experience with the
Semitic Hyksos), there is no recorded case of anti-Semitism until
Haman's attempt to wipe out the Jews of the Persian Empire in
the fifth century B.C.E. This instance, whose historicity has, to be
sure, been contested, was apparently exceptional, since the policy
of the Persian Empire was generally one of toleration toward its
many minorities, an attitude undoubtedly dictated by the fact
that the ruling Persians were a relatively small minority in their
vast realm. The destruction of the temple of the Jewish mercen-
aries at Elephantine in southern Egypt in 411 should be regarded
not as anti-Semitism but as revenge by the native Egyptians
against the hated Persian rulers whose interests had been represented by these Jews for two centuries.

With Alexander (356–323 B.C.E.) a new era dawned for the
Jews; they were now encouraged to settle in the cities that he
established, most notably Alexandria in Egypt. Although he
sought the spread of the Greek language and culture, Alexander
was enough of a realist to understand that he could not rule
his vast, newly acquired empire containing so few Greeks and
Macedonians unless he continued to be tolerant of native peoples.
He and his successors in Egypt, the Ptolemies, realized that they
would never be able to control the native Egyptians, who still
remembered their glorious kingdom of the past, unless they could
count on a group of "middlemen," a position readily filled by the
Jews. From the Jewish point of view, this "vertical" alliance with
their rulers which, of course, was not unique to the Jews but
extended to other minorities, likewise appeared advantageous.
Within a very short period Alexandria had displaced Athens as
the cultural and commercial center of the Mediterranean world,

and the Jews flocked to the city in large numbers. The self-rule granted to them and their ability to enter various fields, including (perhaps because of their higher literacy) the civil service as well as the army, served as considerable inducements.

It was their successful "meddling" in politics and their loyalty to the ruler in power that helped to inspire charges that the Jews were not truly loyal to the best interests of the state. Ironically, an early report by Hecataeus (ca. 300 B.C.E.) noted that it was precisely in recognition of the loyalty shown by the Jews that Alexander the Great added to their territory the district of Samaria free of tribute.[4] Josephus emphasized that the Ptolemies in Egypt later trusted the Jews because of their extraordinary constancy in keeping oaths and pledges. Indeed, Ptolemy VI Philometor (181–145 B.C.E.) placed his entire army under the command of two Jews, and Cleopatra III, the wife of Ptolemy VII Physcon, shortly thereafter entrusted her army to two Jewish generals.[5] Jewish military influence, however, could be a mixed blessing; in 145 B.C.E., a massacre of Alexandrian Jews appears to have been prompted by the fact that the commander-in-chief of the Ptolemaic army, the Jew Onias, had taken sides in a dynastic war.[6]

Apparently the Jews of Egypt retained their religious ties with their brethren in the land of Israel; and this led to the recurring charge, so often found against Jews throughout the ages, that divided loyalties made them less than exemplary citizens of the countries in which they happened to reside. Apion, in accordance with the ancient view that participation in the civic religion was an indication of good citizenship, asked why, if the Jews were citizens, they did not worship the same gods as the Alexandrians; and he proceeded to accuse the Jews of fostering sedition while they were in notorious concert one with the other.[7] This charge of double loyalty may well have been fostered by three incidents in the Jewish experience.[8]

The first occurred about 102 B.C.E. when Cleopatra III heeded the warning of her Jewish commander-in-chief that an invasion of Judaea would turn all the Jews into her enemies. In 55 B.C.E., Jewish soldiers guarding the Egyptian frontier were persuaded by the ruler of Judaea to allow a Roman proconsul to enter Egypt, and seven years later they again submitted to Judaean pressure and allowed an army of Caesar's allies to cross the frontier unmolested. Thus, although our sources provide no specifics for Apion's accusation, the context of his charge is not altogether obscure.

As to the Seleucids of Syria, they likewise maintained the tradition of the Persians and of Alexander in permitting religious tolerance. After the Seleucids had conquered Palestine in 198 B.C.E., they apparently feared that the Palestinian Jews might favor the Ptolemies, under whose moderate rule they had lived since Alexander's death; consequently, we find that the Syrian ruler Antiochus III gave special privileges to the Jews. He exempted them from all taxation for three years and then reduced their tax burden by a third, while exempting the priests, the freedmen, and the members of the Jewish governing body from all taxes. The infamous and atypical persecution of the Jews of Judaea by Antiochus IV Epiphanes can hardly be regarded as straightforward anti-Semitism, especially when we realize that, as far as we know, Antiochus did not persecute the Jews in the other parts of his realm; the struggle in Judaea should rather be viewed as a civil war between Jewish factions.[9]

Under the Romans, the Jews maintained and even strengthened their vertical alliance with the ruling power. At the outset it was in the Roman interest to support the Maccabean rebellion against the rule of the Syrian Greeks, Rome's chief rival in the eastern Mediterranean, and, in fact, Judah Maccabee contracted an alliance with the Romans. Moreover, as Judaism spread through the next two centuries, the realistic Romans no doubt perceived that the Jews were too numerous (perhaps 10 per cent of the population of the Roman Empire as a whole during the reign of Augustus[10] and 20 per cent of the eastern half of the Empire) to risk antagonizing.

There is one significant report of an expulsion of Jews from the city of Rome itself in 139 B.C.E. as a reaction against Jewish efforts to attract pagans to Judaism or Jewish rites.[11] Such an expulsion, however, must have been short-lived, since by the following century the Jewish presence in Rome was noted bitterly by such writers as Cicero and Horace. Indeed, it is of special interest that the law of 65 B.C.E. that demanded the general expulsion of all non-citizens from Rome does not seem to have affected the Jews, since a few years later, in 59 B.C.E., Cicero noted "how numerous they are, their clannishness, and their influence in the assemblies."[12] Cicero was defending a client, and lawyers have been known to exaggerate, but it is self-evident that this courtroom tactic was possible only in a city with a Jewish community of some visibility and at least a modicum of influence.

Shortly after Cicero's remarks, the standing of the Jews in the Empire was enhanced significantly by no less a figure than Julius Caesar himself. Caesar, whose actions served as weighty precedents in the eyes of his successors, was grateful for Jewish assistance rendered during his civil war with Pompey, and he consequently granted the Jews numerous privileges. In city after city in Asia Minor, decrees were issued exempting the Jews from military service, permitting them to send money to the Temple in Jerusalem, and allowing them to form corporate groups, a concession granted uniquely to the Jews that must have seemed remarkable to the non-Jewish inhabitants. Not surprisingly, such preferential treatment did not leave intercommunal relations unscathed. The fact that no fewer than eight cities in Asia Minor were pressured by the Romans to stop their harassment of the Jews (if we assume, as most scholars do, that the Roman documents are authentic) indicates that such privileges were deeply resented.

Relations between Jews and the Roman authorities were not, of course, without grave and ultimately explosive tensions, but before the great revolt of 66–74 C.E. even the most serious incidents were relatively short-lived. In 19 C.E. 4,000 Jews were reportedly expelled from Rome after Jewish embezzlers defrauded a noble proselyte.[13] As in the earlier expulsion, there is reason to believe that Jewish conversionary activity played a role in this decision;[14] in any event, the banishment was brief, it was connected with the activities of a particularly notorious anti-Semite, and it is even possible that it affected only proselytes.[15] The later attempt by Caligula to force the Jews to worship him was regarded as the act of a madman, and despite an enigmatic remark by Suetonius, it appears highly unlikely that Claudius ever expelled them from Rome.[16]

In the land of Israel, the pressures that led to revolution cannot be perceived in the main as a result of anti-Semitism, although some of the special characteristics of Judaism certainly contributed both to Jewish resistance and to Roman irritation and repression. In the crucial decades before the revolt Jews were often successful in pressing appeals to the governor of Syria and even the emperor himself, and there are various indications that Jewish influence in the royal court was not negligible.[17] Still more striking is the Roman failure to reverse the policy of toleration even after the conclusion of the bloody and unsuccessful revolt. It is true that the Temple tax was converted into the humiliating *fiscus Iudaicus* for the upkeep of the temple of Jupiter and that this tax was collected very strictly, especially during the reign of Domitian (81–96 C.E.).[18] Nevertheless, immediately after the revolt, a number of indications point to the fact that Jewish influence remained in high places: The Jewish king Agrippa II was given the rank of praetor, his sister Berenice became the mistress of the Emperor Titus himself, and the historian Josephus was given a pension and a residence in the former mansion of the emperor.

After the death of Domitian, there was again a relaxation of anti-Jewish pressure, and even the great Diaspora revolt of 115–117 C.E. does not appear to have caused fundamental changes in Roman policy. Finally, the Hadrianic prohibition of circumcision, which probably precipitated the Bar-Kokhba revolt of 132–135 c.e., was not directed only against Jews; the revolt itself was, of course, followed by a series of draconian decrees against many Jewish observances, but these too were alleviated by Hadrian's immediate successor.

The essential toleration extended to the Jews does not go unappreciated in rabbinic literature. It is hardly necessary to point out that various rabbinic comments denounced Rome as a wicked kingdom, but these were balanced in part by a significant number of favorable remarks. Esau's descendants were rewarded for his filial piety,[19] the founding of Rome was placed even earlier than it is by Roman tradition itself,[20] and Roman justice was cited with admiration as a central reason for God's positive evaluation of His own act of creation.[21]

None of this should obscure the fact that the Jews, alone among all the subjects of the Empire, erupted into revolt three times between the middle of the first and the middle of the second centuries. This is hardly the symptom of an idyllic relationship. Nevertheless, the revolts were not the norm. They took place against the backdrop of an essentially tolerant policy that was a manifestation, at least in the Diaspora, of a vertical alliance between Jews and the government. It is especially striking that even in revolt Jews did not appear to have sought horizontal alliances with other oppressed people. Relations between Jews and the Roman government were marked by alliance, persecution, and revolt, but it is the alliance that was dominant. Government anti-Semitism was not a significant phenomenon in the ancient world.

Popular Anti-Semitism

When we turn to the attitudes of the masses, the picture changes radically. We do not, of course, possess any writings by ordinary people except for a few fragments of papyri, and the intellectuals who produced our literary sources generally express the utmost contempt for the mob. Nevertheless, the sources leave no room for doubt about the widespread hatred and fear of Jews among the masses in the Roman Empire.

We have already noted that the Roman government had to prevent various cities in Asia Minor from interfering with Jewish observance,[22] but such local persecution was but a mild expression of popular anti-Semitism. The hatred of the mob came into boldest relief during a series of riots that can legitimately be described as anti-Semitic pogroms.

The first of these took place in Alexandria in the year 38 C.E. Philo reported that when the Jews refused to obey Caligula's decree that he be worshipped as a god, the promiscuous mob gave full expression to its long-smoldering hatred of the Jews.[23] Ralph Marcus has already noted that this riot illustrates a typical pattern of ancient pogroms:[24] first, long-standing resentment at the privileged position and influence of the Jews, whether political or economic; second and more immediate, the accusation that the Jews were unpatriotic, inasmuch as they refused to participate in the state cults, which, like a flag, united all the diverse peoples of the Empire; third, the rousing of the passions of the mob by professional agitators (though this is perhaps exceptional); fourth, the intervention of the government to preserve order while blaming the Jews for causing the riot. In the case of the riot of 38 C.E., there were additional, special circumstances. Even with the mad Caligula as emperor, the pogrom was hardly inevitable, since the Jewish king Agrippa I had so much influence with the emperor and since Caligula himself had attributed Jewish recalcitrance to stupidity rather than evil. What determined the course of events in this instance was the behavior of Flaccus, the Roman governor of Egypt.

In the first five of the six years of his administration, Flaccus was a model administrator who showed no sign of anti-Jewish animus. Philo conjectured that the change in attitude reflected during the pogrom of 38 C.E. resulted from transformations in the Roman administration that made Flaccus insecure about his standing with the emperor.

The immediate pretext for the riot was the visit of Agrippa I to Alexandria and his ostentatious display of his bodyguard of spearmen, decked in armor overlaid with gold and silver. To the envious anti-Semites this highlighted Jewish wealth and power. The mob responded by dressing up a lunatic named Carabas in mock-royal apparel with a crown and bodyguards and saluting him as "Marin," the Aramaic for "lord." The implied charge was that the Alexandrian Jews, in giving homage to Agrippa as a king, were actually guilty of dual loyalty and of constituting themselves, in effect, as a state within a state. It may even be that the use of the Aramaic word was intended to emphasize the allegation that the Jews' first loyalty was to the Aramaic-speaking ruler of Palestine. Flaccus's response was not merely to seize the meeting house of the Jews but also to deprive them of civic rights, to denounce them as foreigners and as aliens, and to herd them into a very small part of one of the quarters of the city, the first ghetto in history. Ancient writers rarely stressed or even indicated economic causes of events, and this riot was no exception; nevertheless, the fact that the anti-Semites then pillaged Jewish homes and shops with abandon may indicate that economic considerations were far from insignificant. Indeed, one immediate result of the pogrom was the mass unemployment that occurred because Jewish merchants, artisans, and shipmen lost their stocks and were not allowed to practice their usual business. The sheer savagery of the anti-Semitic mob in binding Jews alive, burning them slowly with brushwood, dragging them through the middle of the marketplace, jumping on them, and not sparing even their dead bodies further indicates the release of pent-up fury reminiscent of the massacres of Polish Jews in the seventeenth century.

Flaccus, according to Philo, could have halted the pogrom in an hour if he had desired, but did nothing. Once they knew that the governmental authority would take no action, the mob attacked the synagogues and placed portraits of Caligula in all of them, while Flaccus himself made a special point of arresting the members of the Gerousia, the body of Jews responsible for their self-government, and stripped and scourged them. Both of these acts were intended to underscore Jewish separatism and lack of patriotism, and the fact that the Jews were accused of storing arms—an accusation that was disproved when absolutely nothing was found—may be an indication that the Jews were perceived as plotting a revolution, perhaps in conjunction with Palestinian revolutionaries. In the end, what must have seemed to the anti-Semites like an instance of "international Jewish power" asserted itself: Flaccus was recalled in disgrace, banished, and eventually executed.[25]

The next major eruption of anti-Jewish violence coincided with the outbreak of the Jewish revolution against the Romans in 66 C.E. Not unexpectedly, this most violent of all the outbreaks occurred in Alexandria with its long history of enmity toward Jews on the part of both Greeks and native Egyptians. Their hostility, which had been generated in part by the combination of equal rights and special privileges granted to Jews, exploded into serious rioting once word of the Judaean revolt arrived. Presumably, the anti-Semites felt assured that the authorities would favor their cause against people who would now be perceived as unpatriotic rebels and who were greeted on at least one occasion by shouts of "enemies" and "spies."

When a mob seized three Jews with the intention of burning them alive, the whole Jewish community rose to their rescue; a riot resulted. The riot was put down ruthlessly by the Roman governor Tiberius Julius Alexander, an apostate Jew, whose troops reportedly killed 50,000 Jews. The fact that the Romans were not without casualties would seem to indicate that at least some Jews were armed, and the fury of the Roman assault, which knew no pity even for infants, would seem to indicate that these Jews fought tenaciously. As for the mob itself, so intense was its hatred that considerable effort was required to tear the attackers from the corpses.[26]

In the land of Israel as well, the friction between the Jews and the non-Jews was evidently of long standing. Philo, for example, remarked that the inhabitants of Ascalon had a certain implacable and irreconcilable enmity to the Jewish inhabitants of the Holy Land with whom they shared a frontier.[27] It should not be surprising, therefore, that at the outbreak of the war the non-Jewish inhabitants of Ascalon killed 2,500 Jews, while in a number of other cities the Jews were expelled, imprisoned, or slain.[28]

A similar indication of a long-simmering hostility is to be seen in the remark of the commander of Masada that the non-Jews had always been quarreling with the Jewish residents of Caesarea and that they seized the opportunity at the outbreak of the war to satisfy their "ancient hate."[29] This feeling had manifested itself earlier upon the death of Agrippa I, when the non-Jewish inhabitants of Caesarea and Samaria hurled indecent insults at him and celebrated feasts, presumably reflecting their resentment at the political power that the Jews had gained when he had been named king by the Romans, and this despite the benefactions that he had bestowed upon them.[30] Indeed, Josephus made a point of indicating that the immediate cause of the revolt of 66 C.E. was the arrival of a rescript from the Emperor Nero to the disputing parties at Caesarea giving control of the city to the Greeks, thus presumably signaling to the Jews the breakdown of the vertical alliance with the authorities in Rome.[31]

Josephus noted that the non-Jewish inhabitants of Caesarea slaughtered the Jews of that city at the very same hour that the Roman garrison in Herod's palace in Jerusalem was massacred. The break in the tie between the Jews and their rulers meant that the anti-Semitic mobs were, in effect, given *carte blanche* throughout the Empire for their murderous assaults. Indeed, it was presumably the fact that the Romans ceased to act as "honest brokers" between the two groups and instead favored the non-

Jews that led the Jews to the painful conclusion that they could no longer count on the vertical alliance with their rulers to protect them. In any event, the fact that 20,000 Jews were slaughtered in Caesarea within one hour (a kind of Jewish St. Bartholemew's Day in more concentrated form, even if the figure is an exaggeration) indicates the premeditated nature and ferocity of the assault. This, in turn, set in motion a series of reprisals by Jews against non-Jews in a number of Palestinian and Syrian villages and cities, after which the Syrians retaliated with a massacre of Jews.[32]

Significantly, Josephus cited the presence of "Judaizers" in each Syrian city;[33] and one may guess that one of the causes of the Jew-hatred was precisely the Jewish success in winning converts and gaining "sympathizers," as well as the eagerness of the Jews to expand their civic rights. Josephus himself ascribed three motives to the anti-Semites: hatred, fear, and greed for plunder.[34] Josephus's declaration that the Jews of Caesarea were superior in wealth and physical strength is especially revealing.[35] One may reasonably infer that Jewish wealth created jealousy; and, indeed, we find that when the procurator Felix let loose his soldiers against the Caesarean Jews, he permitted his troops to plunder certain houses of the Jewish inhabitants that were laden with very large sums of money.[36] Finally, by pointing to the Jews' physical strength, Josephus was doubtless including their sheer number; and we may surmise that the non-Jews were frightened by the increase in the Jewish population[37] that resulted at least in part from success in proselytism.

Despite this series of disasters, it is striking that the Jews could ultimately count on the support of the rulers against the mob. Antioch was one of only three Syrian cities that, according to Josephus, had not indulged in popular anti-Semitic massacres of the Jews on the eve of the war. After the outbreak of the fighting, however, the security of the Jews was ended, and a renegade Jew named Antiochus incited a riot when he accused the Jews of planning to burn the city. Now that the revolution had broken out in Judaea, the Roman general no longer protected the

Louis H. Feldman

Jews and instead sent troops to aid Antiochus in forcing the Jews to violate the Sabbath. Nevertheless, when Antiochus incited a second attack after the capture of Jerusalem, the results were quite different. Once the revolt of the Jews in Jerusalem was over, the Roman administrator restrained the fury of the mob. Shortly thereafter, when the victorious Roman general Titus passed through Antioch, the non-Jewish population greeted him enthusiastically and petitioned him to expel the Jews from the city. Titus, however, was unmoved by this request and listened in silence. When the people of the city persisted, Titus declined, stating that since the country of the Jews had been destroyed, they had nowhere to go. When the people asked that at least the privileges of the Jews should be removed, Titus again refused, leaving the status of the Jews as it formerly was.[38]

The bitterness of mob hatred and also ultimate Roman protectiveness were illustrated once again in the great Diaspora revolt of 115 C.E., which was led by the pseudo-Messiah Lukuas-Andreas. Dio Cassius, who elsewhere expressed respect for the sincere religiosity of the Jews, nevertheless declared that they "would eat the flesh of their victims, make belts for themselves out of their entrails, anoint themselves with their blood and wear their skins for clothing; many they sawed in two, from the head downwards; others they gave to wild beasts, and still others they forced to fight as gladiators."[39] The reports of such atrocities illustrate the extreme bitterness that the Jews' opponents felt toward them; and the fact that, according to Dio, the atrocities were carried out against both Romans and Greeks indicates that the local Greek population must have borne the brunt of the fury of the Jews. Our sources, both literary and papyrological, all emanate from non-Jewish sources and are one-sided. One papyrus relates how the whole peasantry in an Egyptian district took the field against the Jews. Eighty years after the revolt the people of Oxyrhynchos celebrated an annual festival commemorating the victory over the Jews in which they had helped the Roman army. In another of the papyri an irascible old lady prays to the invincible Hermes to preserve her son from being roasted, apparently by the Jews (though the Jews are not explicitly mentioned).[40] We do not know the causes, alleged or otherwise, of the hatred felt by the non-Jews toward the Jews and vice versa; but we may guess that the messianic character of the revolt is a major clue, and that the Jews may have sought to establish an independent state, under a messianic king, stretching from Cyrene and Egypt to Cyprus, Palestine, and Mesopotamia, all of which were scenes of revolt. The fact that the revolt lasted for three years (115–117 C.E.) and was so fierce indicates that the fear that the Jews might establish such a state was not without foundation. We may infer from one papyrus that after the Roman victory over the Jews, Greeks in Alexandria, mainly slaves, started an anti-Jewish uprising upon the instigation of people of influence.[41] Once again, however, it was the Roman administration which, despite the rebellion of the Jews, took measures against the Greek troublemakers in order to re-establish law and order. Still, the Jewish community of Egypt had been decimated by these events and was not to be reconstituted in strength until the medieval period.

In Rome itself, despite the insinuations about Jewish clannishness and influence in Cicero's defense of Flaccus, there was apparently no history of virulent anti-Semitism on the part of the mob, noted though it was for its size and unruly nature. We may conjecture that this may have been because the Jews in the city, unlike those in Alexandria or Antioch or Caesarea, did not have or seek special political privileges, so far as we know. Moreover, the fact that Rome was the seat of the emperor, who had regarded himself since the days of Julius Caesar as the protector of the Jews, may have served as a deterrent. Finally, because the emperor constantly had has own bodyguard and a sizable number of troops in readiness to protect him from assassination or violent outbreaks, such popular uprisings would have been difficult to carry out.

Louis H. Feldman

Intellectual Anti-Semitism

Though it is perhaps hard for us to imagine a time when the world was not preoccupied with the "Jewish question," for many centuries in antiquity this was the case. Thus it is not until Herodotus in the fifth century B.C.E. that any extant Greek writer mentioned the Jews at all, and the first mention of them was oblique, in a discussion of circumcision.[42] Stern's monumental three-volume collection of testimonia to the Jews in pagan writers[43] seems large, but the truth is that many of the quotations deal only peripherally with the Jews as such. Indeed, if Josephus's reply *Against Apion* had been lost, we would be lacking a large proportion of the most virulent anti-Semitic texts.

Scholars who have examined this corpus have emphasized the almost universal prevalence of virulent anti-Semitism in the remarks of these writers. In Germany it became fashionable to cite these passages in promoting the thesis that the Jew's inherent characteristics produced anti-Semitism wherever he went, especially among men of intellectual attainments. And yet, as I have tried to indicate elsewhere,[44] Jews were admired as possessing the four cardinal virtues of wisdom, courage, temperance, and justice; and the list of their admirers included figures of the stature of Aristotle, his successor Theophrastus, and Varro, who was to be termed by the great literary critic Quintilian "the most learned of the Romans." Indeed, one of antiquity's most distinguished literary critics, the first-century pseudo-Longinus, praises the opening of Genesis as an example of the most lofty style.[45] Moreover, many of the hostile passages come from rhetorical historians or satirists, where the references are clearly colored and exaggerated. In addition, other peoples of antiquity, such as the Egyptians, Syrians, Thracians, Spaniards, Gauls, Germans, Phrygians, and Carthaginians, as well as the Greeks and Romans themselves, are also objects of detestation and derision. Thus, for example, two of the charges made against Jews, that they are lazy and superstitious, were also made by Tacitus against the Germans. The fact that so many pagans embraced Judaism during this period shows that Jews were by no means universally unpopular and that they had more contacts with non-Jews than is generally recognized. Finally, according to my own count, 101 (18 per cent) of the comments by pagans in Stern's collection are substantially favorable, 339 (59 per cent) are more or less neutral, and only 130 (23 per cent) are substantially unfavorable.[46] Nonetheless, it must be granted that a number of serious charges are made by the intellectual anti-Semites, and it would be useful to discuss them briefly.

1. HATRED OF MANKIND   Though the Torah (Exodus 23:9) commands the Jew to treat the stranger with respect, the dietary laws, Sabbath laws, and rules regarding idolatry were formidable barriers that prevented the Jews from fraternizing with Gentiles. The fact that Gentiles were forbidden to enter the Temple precinct and the prohibition against teaching Gentiles the Torah may likewise have contributed to rumors and to misunderstanding, including a blood libel.[47] Thus Josephus's version of King Solomon's prayer at the dedication of the Temple specifically denies that the Jews are "inhumane by nature or unfriendly to those who are not of our country," and declares that they "wish that all men equally should receive aid from Thee and enjoy Thy blessings."[48] The significance of this issue is underscored by the fact that even Hecataeus, who was well disposed toward the Jews, characterized the Jewish mode of life as somewhat unsocial and hostile to foreigners (*misoxenon*). This is the sole remark in his account that may be termed negative, though even it is qualified by the word "somewhat" and justified as a reaction to the Jews' expulsion from Egypt.[49] Nevertheless, the term *misoxenon* is clearly hostile, as we see from the fact that the sole occurrence of the word other than in this passage is in Josephus, where it refers to the hatred of foreigners exhibited by the despised people of Sodom.[50]

This perception of the Jews is found in a host of other

Louis H. Feldman

writings as well. Apollonius Molon condemned the Jews for illiberalism in that they refuse admission to persons with other ideas about God and will not associate with those who have adopted a different manner of life. Diodorus similarly reported that when King Antiochus Sidetes was laying siege to Jerusalem, the majority of his friends advised him to wipe out the Jews, "since they alone of all nations avoided dealings with any other people and looked upon all men as their enemies"; this hatred of mankind, they said, went back to the expulsion from Egypt and was demonstrated most clearly by the Jewish refusal to break bread with any other race or to show them any good will at all. Pompeius Trogus similarly connected the Jews' alleged misanthropy with their expulsion from Egypt, remarking that they had adopted such an attitude in order to avoid again becoming odious to their neighbors. Lysimachus reflected the charge of misanthropy when he remarked that Moses instructed the Israelites to show good will to no man, to offer not the best but the worst advice, and to overthrow the temples and altars of the gods. Apion, in his malice, went further, attributing to the Jews an oath to show no good will to any alien, especially to Greeks. The philosopher Euphrates was quoted by Philostratus as noting that the Jews do not mingle with others in common meals, libations, prayers, or sacrifices.[51]

Many of the laws that engendered Jewish separatism were themselves subjected to ridicule by Greek and Roman intellectuals. The Roman fondness for pork made the Jewish dietary regulations particularly vulnerable to mockery; circumcision was perceived as an outright abomination; the Sabbath laws were distorted to include abstention not only from work but also from food; and the worship of a single, imageless God was virtually incomprehensible to many ancient thinkers.[52]

Among the Romans, Cicero was particularly resentful, at least by implication, of the Jewish claim to enjoy divine protection, presumably as the chosen people of God, when he declares sarcastically, "The nation (i.e., the Jews) . . . has made it clear

how far it enjoys divine protection by the fact that it has been conquered, scattered, enslaved."[53] Similarly, Celsus alluded sarcastically to the "Promised Land" by remarking: "We see what
sort of land it was of which they (i.e., the Jews) were thought
worthy."[54]

Tacitus accused the Jews of regarding the rest of mankind
with all the hatred of enemies, and in immediate juxtaposition he
gave the apparent source of this conception: They sit and sleep
apart from other peoples and abstain from intercourse with
foreign women.[55] Juvenal, in his bitter satirical tone, condemned
the Jews for not showing the way or pointing out a fountain
spring to anyone who is not circumcised. It may be that the
allusion here is to the prohibition to show the way (that is, to
teach the Torah) to Gentiles, a prohibition that may have given
non-Jews the impression that Judaism was a mystery cult; the
reference to circumcision and a fountain may allude to the two
most prominent features of the Jewish conversion ceremony.[56]

Josephus clearly answered the charge that the Jews are mis-
anthropes when he said that the Greeks, too, were opposed to
foreigners; in particular, he cited the Spartan practice of expelling
foreigners and not allowing citizens to travel abroad. In contrast
to this, said Josephus, the Jews gladly welcome proselytes, thus
affording a proof of their humanity and magnanimity. It appears
that Josephus similarly answered the charge that the Jews do not
point out the way to non-Jews when he remarked that the Torah
prescribes sharing fire, water, and food with others when they ask
for them, and that the Jew is commanded to point out the road to
non-Jews.[57]

2. CREDULITY   To the Greeks, credulity was an embarrassment.
Herodotus criticized the Athenians for allowing themselves to be
deceived by a crude ruse, and he noted that the Greeks since
olden times had been far removed from ridiculous simplicity and
had been distinguished from others by their cleverness.[58]

In view of the nature of talmudic discussions (admittedly

later but reflecting earlier methodology), which put a premium upon critical questioning, it seems surprising that the Jews should have had a reputation for credulity. The generally sympathetic Hecataeus remarked that the Jews were so docile that they fell to the ground and paid homage to the high priest when he expounded the commandments to them. Greeks, presumably, would have questioned such rules.[59] The same characteristic was mentioned derisively by Mnaseas of Patara in Asia Minor (ca. 200 B.C.E.), who, according to Apion, told how the Jews were deceived by the Idumaean stratagem reminiscent of the ruse that misled the Athenians.[60] Finally, this same credulity was alluded to by Horace, who said that only the proverbial Jew Apella would believe that frankincense can melt without fire. Horace, like the Epicureans, professed that the gods do not intervene in human affairs and thus do not perform such miracles.[61]

3. JEWS AS BEGGARS   Perhaps because of the traditional Jewish emphasis on works of charity, the Jews seem to have attracted many proselytes who realized that by becoming Jews they were assured of food and lodging. Lysimachus, the arch–anti-Semite, made retroactive this association of the Jews with beggars when he declared that after the exodus of the leprous Jews from Egypt, they lived a mendicant existence.[62]

To the epigrammist Martial at the end of the first century, the Jew taught by his mother to beg was a proverbial figure among the many nuisances in the city of Rome. It was the satirist Juvenal who poured the most scorn upon Jewish begging, noting bitterly that a formerly holy grove had been let out to Jews if they had some straw and a basket, so that the forest was swarming with beggars. Later he described a beggar as hanging out in some synagogue with Jews, and elsewhere he spoke of a Jewess leaving her basket and hay and soliciting alms, while playing on the credulity of others by telling fortunes and interpreting dreams.[63]

4. DOUBLE LOYALTY   We have already examined the accusation of double loyalty that appears to be implicit in a number of classical sources. It should be noted here that Apion not only accused the Jews of sedition and failure to worship the civic deities, but also expressed astonishment that they were called Alexandrians.[64] In answer to Apion's charge that the Jews promote sedition, Josephus stated that the real promoters of sedition were the native Egyptians, whereas the Jews were remarkable for their harmony, a quality admitted to be present in Jews by two other anti-Semites, Cicero and Tacitus.[65]

We may conjecture that the charge of double loyalty was also a factor in a well-documented court case. Cicero's client Flaccus seized money that the Jews of Asia Minor sought to ship out of the province to the Temple in Jerusalem. This may well have seemed unpatriotic to the Romans because of the scarcity of money at this time throughout the Empire. Indeed, in 63 B.C.E., four years before the trial, the Senate had passed a resolution forbidding the export of gold and silver from Italy because of the shortage; and Flaccus had sent the Jewish money to Rome for deposit in the public treasury. Thus Cicero took care to imply that the Jews were unpatriotic,[66] and he urged the jury to show their concern for the welfare of the state and to despise the Jewish pressure group.

5. AGGRESSIVENESS IN PROSELYTISM   There is much evidence to indicate the success of Jewish missionary activities. Strabo spoke of the conversion of the Idumaeans to Judaism during the reign of John Hyrcanus, though he did not indicate that it was by compulsion, as did Ptolemy and Josephus. In fact, elsewhere Strabo stressed that Moses attracted neighboring peoples to Judaism through the reputation that he enjoyed and through the kind of government that he had established.[67]

Horace spoke of the missionary zeal of the Jews as something proverbial: "We, like the Jews, will compel you to join our

34   Louis H. Feldman

throng."[68] Though satirists exaggerate, the point would have been lost if there had not been considerable basis to it.

We have already noted the report that the Jews were banished from Rome in 139 B.C.E. because they had attempted "to transmit their sacred rites to the Romans."[69] Seneca apparently alluded to the success of Jewish proselytism when he said that the customs of the Jews have gained such influence that "they are now received throughout the world," and the vanquished have thus given laws to their victors (*victi victoribus leges dederunt*).[70] Elsewhere he made an oblique reference to the persecution of the Jewish and Egyptian rites by Tiberius, apparently for attempting to proselytize. ("Some foreign rites were at that time being inaugurated, and abstinence from certain kinds of animal foods was set down as a proof of interest in the strange cult.")[71]

Epictetus, who recognized that full conversion to Judaism requires ritual immersion, referred to those who act the part of a Jew (presumably "sympathizers" with Judaism) when they actually were not yet converted, and he went on to note the apparent confrontation between Judaism and Stoicism: "Why, then, do you call yourself a Stoic? Why do you deceive the multitude? Why do you act the part of a Jew when you are a Greek?"[72] (Apparently, the latter point was so common that it gave rise to a proverb: "He is not a Jew; he is only acting the part.") It is noteworthy that many of those, such as Seneca, Persius, and Juvenal, who were most bitter against the Jews, were either Stoics or strongly influenced by Stoicism, and this may reflect the intense competition for converts during the early Roman Empire.

Tacitus bitterly alluded to the missionary zeal of the Jews, noting that the most degraded of other races, scorning the peoples of their origin, brought to the Jews their contributions and gifts, thus augmenting the Jews' wealth. He noted that those who join the Jewish fold despise all the gods, disown their country, and disregard their families, which may be an allusion to the fact that a proselyte to Judaism is legally regarded as one who has no relatives.[73] To Roman intellectuals such illiberalism toward other religions was inexcusable. To the intelligentsia it was precisely the unwillingness of Jews to engage in meaningful contact with other religious groups on a plane of equality—a *sine qua non* for the intellectual who welcomes debate and, at least in theory, expresses a readiness to adopt another point of view if it can be shown to be superior to his own—that proved the Jews were obscurantists. Josephus provided an apologetic reaction to this perception by having Abraham descend to Egypt to an international scientific congress, so to speak, in which the loser of the debate agrees to adopt the philosophic position of the winner.[74] The intellectuals could not understand the illiberalism of the Jews in failing to accord respect to the religions of others,[75] and hence the efforts of the Septuagint, Philo, and Josephus to show, on the basis of an interpretation of Exodus 22:27, that Jews are actually commanded to show such respect.[76]

Conclusion

During the Hellenistic and Roman periods, the Jews encountered hostility from governments, mobs, and intellectuals. The anti-Semitism of the last group was by no means universal; and in no case, with the exception of one or possibly two incidents at Alexandria, do we find that intellectuals had any influence in arousing the masses against the Jews, so great, apparently, was the gulf between these teachers and the masses. Indeed, this lack of communication between the intellectuals and the mob may explain why the blood libel, which is found in ancient writings as early as the beginning of the first century, was apparently never an occasion for a pogrom. Nevertheless, there is a good deal of evidence that the anti-Semitism of the masses was deep-seated and that little was needed to trigger it into violence. It was basically the vertical alliance of the Jews with governments, start-

Louis H. Feldman

ing with the Persians, continuing through Alexander and his successors the Ptolemies and the Seleucids, and further continuing with the Romans that, on the whole, restrained the masses from violent outbreaks. The position of the Jews was certainly strengthened by their sheer numbers, constantly increasing through highly successful proselytism, so that we may even conjecture that if the three great revolts against the Romans had not occurred and if Christianity had not lowered the price of admission, so to speak, Judaism might have become the major religion of the Roman Empire. The masses, however, established a love-hate relationship with the Jews; and many of those who remained unconverted were fearful of the prospect that Judaism would bring about the end of their pagan religions. The governments, with few exceptions, did not wish to antagonize so large and important a group and maintained the privileged position of the Jews.

NOTES

1. Salo W. Baron, *A Social and Religious History of the Jews,* vol. 1 (New York, 1952), p. 194.

2. Jerry L. Daniel, "Anti-Semitism in the Hellenistic-Roman Period," *Journal of Biblical Literature* 98 (1979): 45–65.

3. The literature on ancient anti-Semitism is vast, but this may be an opportune time to re-evaluate the evidence in light of the recent appearance of Menahem Stern's monumental *Greek and Latin Authors on Jews and Judaism,* 3 vols. (Jerusalem, 1974–1984), which supersedes Theodore Reinach, *Textes d'auteurs grecs et romains relatifs au Judaisme* (Paris 1895). Of the many studies in this field, the following deserve special notice: Maurilio Adriani, "Note sull'antisemitismo antico," *Studi e materiali di storia delle Religioni* 36 (1965): 63–98; H. Idris Bell, *Cults and Creeds in Graeco-Roman Egypt* (Liverpool, 1954); Jerry L. Daniel, "Anti-Semitism in the Hellenistic-Roman Period," *Journal of Biblical Literature* 98 (1979): 45–65; S. Davis, *Race-Relations in Ancient Egypt: Greek, Egyptian, Hebrew, Roman* (New York, 1952); Louis H. Feldman, "Philosemitism among Ancient Intellectuals," *Tradition* 1 (1958–59): 27–39; Louis H. Feldman, "The Jews in Greek and Latin Literature," in Menahem Stern, ed., *The Jewish Diaspora in the Second Temple Period (World History of the Jewish People,* vol. 4) (in press); John G.

Gager, *Moses in Greco-Roman Paganism* (Nashville, 1972); N. W. Goldstein, "Cultivated Pagans and Ancient Anti-Semitism," *Journal of Religion* 19 (1939): 346–364; Isaak Heinemann, "Antisemitismus," in August Pauly and Georg Wissowa, eds., *Realencyclopädie der klassischen Altertumswissenschaft,* Suppl. 5 (1931): 3–43; Isaak Heinemann, "The Attitude of the Ancient World toward Judaism," *Review of Religion* 4 (1939–40): 385–400; Jean Juster, *Les Juifs dans l'Empire romain,* 2 vols. (Paris, 1913), esp. vol. 1, pp. 31ff.; George La Piana, "Foreign Groups in Rome during the First Centuries of the Empire," *Harvard Theological Review* 20 (1927): 183–403; J. Leipoldt, *Antisemitismus in der alten Welt* (Leipzig, 1933); Ralph Marcus, "Antisemitism in the Hellenistic-Roman World," in Koppel S. Pinson, ed., *Essays in Anti-semitism,* 2nd ed. (New York, 1946), pp. 61–78; Arnaldo Momigliano, "Juifs et Grecs," in Léon Poliakov, ed., *Ni Juif ni Grec; entretiens sur le racisme* (Paris, 1978) pp. 47–63; Max Radin, *The Jews among the Greeks and Romans* (Philadelphia, 1915), pp. 76–89, 163–256; Jacob S. Raisin, *Gentile Reactions to Jewish Ideals* (New York, 1953); Jan N. Sevenster, *The Roots of Pagan Anti-Semitism in the Ancient World* (Leiden, 1975); A. N. Sherwin-White, *Racial Prejudice in Imperial Rome* (Cambridge, 1967), esp. pp. 86–101; Menahem Stern, "The Jews in Greek and Latin Literature," in S. Safrai and M. Stern, eds., *The Jewish People in the First Century* (*Compendia Rerum Iudaicarum ad Novum Testamentum,* section 1, vol. 2; Philadelphia, 1976), pp. 1101–1159; Victor Tcherikover, *Hellenistic Civilization and the Jews* (Philadelphia, 1959), pp. 357–377; Robert L. Wilken, "Judaism in Roman and Christian Society," *Journal of Religion* 47 (1967): 313–330; and Solomon Zeitlin, "Anti-Semitism," *Crozer Quarterly* 22 (1945): 134–149. See also John G. Gager, *The Origins of Anti-Semitism: Attitudes Toward Judaism in Pagan and Christian Antiquity* (New York, 1983).

4. See Josephus, *Against Apion* 2. 43.

5. Josephus, *Antiquities* 11. 318, 12. 8; *Against Apion* 2.49; *Antiquities* 13. 349.

6. *Against Apion* 2. 53–54. The narrative in 3 Maccabees 5–6 about a massacre in 217 B.C.E. is suspiciously similar to Josephus's account and is considerably less plausible. See the remarks of H. St. John Thackeray, *Josephus* (Loeb Classical Library, vol. 1 [London, 1926]), p. 314, n. *a.*

7. *Against Apion* 2. 65.

8. See *Antiquities* 13. 353–355, 14. 99, and 14. 131–132.

9. See Tcherikover, *Hellenistic Civilization and the Jews* (note 3), pp. 175–203.

10. Baron, *Social and Religious History of the Jews* 1 (note 1), pp. 370–372.

11. Valerius Maximus 1. 3. 3, epitome of Januarius Nepotianus. There is no persuasive reason to think that this missionary activity was carried on by the delegation of Simon the Hasmonean to Rome (1 Maccabees 14. 24, 15. 25 ff.), as Emil Schürer, *Geschichte des jüdischen Volkes im Zeitalter Jesu*

Christi, vol. 3 (Leipzig, 1911), p. 59, and Harry J. Leon, *The Jews of Ancient Rome* (Philadelphia, 1960), pp. 2ff., have concluded. Indeed, it is hard to believe that the delegation would have risked jeopardizing their political mission by engaging in religious missionary activity.

12. *Pro Flacco* 28. 66.

13. *Antiquities* 18. 81–84; cf. Suetonius, *Tiberius* 36; Dio Cassius 57. 18. 5a; Tacitus, *Annals* 2. 85.

14. Leon, *Jews of Ancient Rome* (note 11), pp. 17–19; Louis H. Feldman, trans., *Josephus* (Loeb Classical Library, vol. 9 [London, 1965]), pp. 60–61.

15. Cf. Philo, *Legatio ad Gaium* 160, and see Ernest L. Abel, "Were the Jews Banished from Rome in 19 A.D.?" *Revue des Etudes Juives* 127 (1968): 383–386.

16. Suetonius, *Claudius* 25. 4; Acts 18. 2. Note esp. Dio Cassius 60. 6. 6, and see Stern, *Greek and Latin Authors* (n. 3), vol. 2, p. 116.

17. *Jewish War* 2. 232–246; *Antiquities* 20. 118–136; *Life* 13–16; *Antiquities* 20. 195. See also Lee I. Levine, "The Jewish-Greek Conflict in First-Century Caesarea," *Journal of Jewish Studies* 25 (1974): 383, n. 15.

18. Suetonius, *Domitian* 12. Even this tax was not imposed uniquely against the Jews, since, as Michael Rostowzew, "Fiscus," *Realencyclopädie der klassischen Altertumswissenschaft* 12 (1909), pp. 2403–2404, has pointed out, a *fiscus Alexandrinus* and a *fiscus Asiaticus* were similarly levied upon the Alexandrians and Asiatics respectively.

19. *Genesis Rabbah* 65: 16–17. Note the importance of filial piety in Vergil's description of Aeneas.

20. *Yer. Avodah Zarah* 1.2 (39c); *Song of Songs Rabbah* 1.6; *Bav. Shabbat* 56b; *Bav. Sanhedrin* 21b; *Sifre Deuteronomy* 52.

21. *Genesis Rabbah* 9. 13. On the attitude of the rabbis toward Rome see Samuel Krauss, *Monumenta Talmudica*, vol. 5: *Geschichte, 1. Teil: Griechen und Römer* (Vienna, 1914); Moses Hadas, "Roman Allusions in Rabbinic Literature," *Philological Quarterly* 8 (1929): 369–387; Samuel Krauss, *Persia and Rome in the Talmud and in the Midrashim* (Hebrew) (Jerusalem, 1948); Isaac Herzog, "Rome in the Talmud and in the Midrash," in his *Judaism: Law and Ethics* (London, 1974), pp. 83–91; Nahum Glatzer, "The Attitude toward Rome in the Amoraic Period," *Proceedings of the Sixth World Congress of Jewish Studies*, vol. 2 (Jerusalem, 1975), pp. 9–19; Geza Vermes, "Ancient Rome in Post-Biblical Jewish Literature," in his *Post-Biblical Jewish Studies* (Leiden, 1975), pp. 215–224; Nicholas R. M. de Lange, "Jewish Attitudes to the Roman Empire," in Peter D. A. Garnsey and C. R. Wittaker, eds., *Imperialism in the Ancient World* (Cambridge, 1978), pp. 255–281; and Gunter Stemberger, "Die Beurteilung Roms in der rabbinischen Literatur," *Aufstieg und Niedergang der römischen Welt* 2. 19. 2 (1979), pp. 338–396.

22. Cf. for example, *Antiquities* 14. 213, 244–246.

23. *Legatio ad Gaium* 120.

24. Marcus, "Antisemitism in the Hellenistic-Roman World" (note 3), p. 72.

25. On this riot and its aftermath, see *In Flaccum,* passim, and cf. *Legatio ad Gaium* 122, 131–132. A report by the sixth-century chronicler Ioannes Malalas (244. 15 ff.) that a similar pogrom took place in Antioch two years later may also indicate how widespread and deep anti-Semitic feelings ran.

26. On these events in Alexandria, see *Jewish War* 2. 487–498.

27. *Legatio ad Gaium* 205.

28. *Jewish War* 2. 477.

29. *Jewish War* 7. 363.

30. *Antiquities* 19. 356–359.

31. *Antiquities* 20. 183–184. See also Uriel Rappaport, "The Relations between Jews and Non-Jews and the Great War against Rome" (Hebrew), *Tarbiẓ* 47 (1977–1978): 1–14, and "Notes on the Causes of the Great Revolt against Rome" (Hebrew), *Cathedra* 8 (1978): 42–46, who stresses the insoluble conflict between Jews and non-Jews, which he traces back to the Hasmonean period, as the major factor leading to the revolt.

32. *Jewish War* 2. 457, 461. Note too the massacre of 13,000 Jews in Scythopolis (Bethshan) described by Josephus in *Jewish War* 2. 466 and 7. 364–365, and *Life* 26.

33. *Jewish War* 2. 463.

34. *Jewish War* 2. 478, 464.

35. *Antiquities* 20. 175 (which refers only to wealth); *Jewish War* 2. 268.

36. *Antiquities* 20. 177.

37. Levine, "The Jewish Greek Conflict" (note 17), p. 382.

38. *Jewish War* 7. 57, 104, 110–111.

39. Dio Cassius, 68. 32. 1–2.

40. *Corpus Papyrorum Judaicarum,* vol. 2, ed. Victor A. Tcherikover and Alexander Fuks (Cambridge, 1960), nos. 438, 450, 437.

41. *Corpus Papyrorum Judaicarum,* no. 435, and cf. Tcherikover's comment, vol. 2, p. 229.

42. For some speculations on the causes of this phenomenon, which cannot be explained by a lack of contact between Greeks and Jews, see Arnaldo Momigliano, *Alien Wisdom: the Limits of Hellenization* (Cambridge, 1975), pp. 76–82. The problem is sharpened by what sometimes seems like the deliberate omission of Jews—even in later periods—from a discussion where some reference would be expected (e.g., Cicero's *De Natura Deorum*).

43. Above, note 3.

44. Feldman, "Philosemitism" (note 3).

45. Quintilian 10. 1. 95; "Longinus," *On the Sublime* 9. 4.

46. The percentages in the two substantive volumes are essentially the same. In volume 1, from Herodotus in the fifth century B.C.E. through

Plutarch in the first century C.E., 47 notices are favorable (16 per cent), 69 are unfavorable (24 per cent), and 165 are neutral (60 per cent). In volume 2, covering the period from the second through the sixth century, 54 are favorable (20 per cent), 61 are unfavorable (21 per cent), and 174 are neutral (59 per cent). From a modern perspective, the absence of racial connotations in these passages is noteworthy.

47. Apion, in Josephus, *Against Apion* 2. 91–96, and Damocritus, in Suidas, s.v.

48. *Antiquities* 8. 117.

49. Diodorus 40. 3. 4.

50. *Antiquities* 1. 194.

51. *Against Apion* 2. 258; Diodorus 34–35. 1. 1; Justin, *Historiae Philippicae* 36, *Epitoma* 2. 15; *Against Apion* 1. 309 and 2. 121; Philostratus, *Life of Apollonius of Tyana* 5. 33.

52. On the dietary laws: Plutarch, *Cicero* 7. 5; Macrobius, *Saturnalia* 2.4. 11; Philo, *Legatio ad Gaium* 361; Juvenal 6. 160. On circumcision: Horace, *Satires* 1. 9. 60; Persius 5. 184; Petronius, *Satyricon* 68. 8; Martial 11. 94. On the Sabbath: *Antiquities* 14. 66; Justin 36. 2. 14; Martial 4. 4; Suetonius, *Augustus* 76. 2; *Against Apion* 1. 209; Strabo 16. 2. 40; Dio Cassius 37. 15. 3. On the Jewish perception of God: Juvenal 14. 97–98; Dio Cassius 37. 17. 2.

53. *Pro Flacco* 67.

54. Origen, *Contra Celsum* 5. 50.

55. *Histories* 5. 1.

56. Juvenal 14. 103–104. On conversion requirements, see the dispute in *Bav. Yevamot* 46 a–b.

57. *Against Apion* 2. 259–261, 211.

58. Herodotus 1. 60.

59. Diodorus 40. 3. 6.

60. *Against Apion* 2. 112–114.

61. *Satires* 1. 5. 97–103.

62. *Against Apion* 1. 305.

63. Martial 12. 57. 1–14; Juvenal 3. 10–16, 296, and 6. 542–547.

64. *Against Apion* 2. 38.

65. *Against Apion* 2. 68; cf. *Pro Flacco* 28.66 and Tacitus, *Histories* 5. 5.

66. *Pro Flacco* 28. 66: "There is no lack of men, as you well know, to stir these fellows up against me and every patriotic citizen." In general, Cicero's description of the Jews as a large and influential pressure group is worth noting in the context of anti-Semitic rhetoric.

67. Strabo 16. 2. 34. 760; Ptolemy in Ammonius, *De Adfinium Vocabulorum Differentia*, no. 243; *Antiquities* 13. 257; Strabo 16. 2. 36. 761.

68. *Satires* 1. 4. 139–143.

69. See note 11.

70. Augustine, *De Civitate Dei* 6. 11.

71. Seneca, *Epistulae Morales* 108. 22; cf. Tacitus, *Annals* 2. 85.

72. Arrian, *Dissertationes* 2. 9. 19–21.

73. *Histories* 5. 5.

74. See Louis H. Feldman, "Abraham the Greek Philosopher in Josephus," *Transactions of the American Philological Association* 99 (1968): 143–156.

75. *Against Apion* 2. 65.

76. The verse prohibits the cursing of God and, according to the Talmud, of judges as well. The Septuagint, however, translates, "Thou shalt not curse *gods*" (*theous* for the Hebrew *elohim*). See also Philo, *De Vita Mosis* 2. 205, and *De Specialibus Legibus* 1. 53; Josephus, *Antiquities* 4. 207, and *Against Apion* 2. 237.

Louis H. Feldman

"Anti-Semitism" in Antiquity:
The Problem of Definition

Shaye J. D. Cohen

One of the most important objectives of the historian is the interpretation of the past on its own terms, and not on the terms of the interpreter. Most historians, however, especially the historians of antiquity, would concede that this goal is often unattainable. Our knowledge of the ancient world is so fragmentary, our documentation so sparse, and our uncertainties so numerous that the temptation to retroject upon antiquity the conditions and attitudes of the modern world is almost irresistible. This generalization is well exemplified by the study of ancient "anti-Semitism."

Nineteenth-century scholars "discovered" that humanity consisted of different races, each with its own characteristics. The classification of languages into Semitic, Indo-European, Hamitic, and other families was transmuted by these scholars into a racial classification of mankind. Hatred of the Jews was "scientifically justifiable" and received the scientific-sounding name "anti-Semitism." During the latter part of the century even those scholars who were not virulent anti-Semites used the hatred of the Jews in Greco-Roman antiquity to "prove" that Christianity was not responsible for anti-Semitism, since even in pre-Christian times the Jews were odious to Indo-Europeans. The fact that the Jews demanded civic equality while refusing to surrender their distinctiveness and peculiar religious practices was the cause of the anti-Jewish riots in Alexandria in 38–39 C.E., claimed these scholars. In addition, the Jews of Egypt were tax collectors and economic middlemen who aroused the righteous anger and jealousy of their hosts. The Jewish troubles in first-century Egypt presaged and justified the unfriendly reception that the Jews were receiving in post-Emancipation Europe. Against this approach Jewish scholars argued that the ancient and the modern hatreds of Judaism were worlds apart (see, for example, the preface of Theodore Reinach to his *Texts of Greek and Roman Authors Concerning Jews and Judaism,* published [in French] in Paris in 1895, when the Dreyfus affair was on the mind of every Frenchman), but the issue was not easily treated on a scholarly basis. Polemics were opposed by apologetics.

Even contemporary scholars, whose interest in ancient "anti-Semitism" is neither polemical nor apologetic, sometimes retroject modern conditions upon antiquity. Some of the charges leveled against the Jews of antiquity (e.g., hatred of outsiders, clannishness) are identical with those heard in modern times, but not all the ancient charges have modern analogues and not all the modern charges have ancient roots. No ancient text assigns an economic motive to the hatred of Jews. The Jews as money-lenders, usurers, tax collectors, exploiters—these are the images of modern, not ancient, anti-Semitism. It was in modern rather than ancient times that the Jews became a prosperous middle class that penetrated the power structure of society and displaced many of the old elites, thereby arousing their hatred. Many ancient authors, especially in Rome, explicitly describe the Jews as poor. Similarly, the ancients did not accuse the Jews of "dual loyalty." Jews were accused of sedition, rebelliousness, and conspiracy, but not of dual loyalty.

The most serious example of retrojection is the very notion of "anti-Semitism." The Greeks and Romans did not have a conception of "race." Their division of humanity into "Greeks" (or "Romans") and "barbarians" was a product not of racism but

Shaye J. D. Cohen

of cultural snobbery (compare the Jewish use of the term *goy,* "Gentile"). Greek and Roman ethnographers knew that the inhabitants of each nation had specific physical and moral characteristics, but these were generally attributed to the effects of various natural phenomena (climate, soil, water, air, and so forth). For example, the blacks ("Ethiopians") were regarded not as a "race" but as people whose skin had been baked by the heat of the sun (see Frank Snowden, *Blacks in Antiquity*). The Greeks and Romans knew nothing of "Semites." Their statements on the Jews and Judaism must be compared with their views of the Egyptians, Syrians, Indians, Germans, and Gauls; with the Roman views of the Greeks; and with the Greek views of the Romans. (J. P. V. D. Balsdon, *Romans and Aliens,* is an excellent recent survey of the subject.) The size of the three volumes of *Greek and Latin Authors on Jews and Judaism,* edited by Menahem Stern, might suggest that the Greeks and Romans were very concerned about the Jews or that the Jews were the only ethnic group of antiquity to have elicited so much comment (both favorable and unfavorable). These conclusions are false. The context of ancient "anti-Semitism" demonstrates that it was not "anti-Semitism" at all.

The use of the term "anti-Semitism" to describe the anti-Judaism of antiquity is not only anachronistic but also misleading. The term conjures up a vision of an irrational and deep-seated hatred of Jews, but it is far from certain that such a hatred ever existed in antiquity. Many Jews imagine that Antiochus Epiphanes, the leaders of the Alexandrian pogroms, and the emperors Titus and Hadrian were motivated by just such a rabid hatred of Judaism, summed up in the rabbinic adage "Esau hates Jacob," but there is room for doubt. Most modern scholars would agree that the destruction of Jerusalem in 70 C.E. was not an "anti-Semitic" act, because the Romans had good reason to do what they did. The Jews rebelled against the state, and the Romans were acting to preserve their empire. The Antiochean and Hadrianic persecutions of Judaism can be similarly understood (at least in part) as the brutal attempts of the state to repress a rebellion that was motivated (at least in part) by religious zeal. Even the Alexandrian pogroms had some justification. As Apion, the leader of the "anti-Semitic" party, asked, "If the Jews wish to become Alexandrian citizens, why don't they worship the Alexandrian gods?"—an excellent question. The Jews wanted equality with tolerance, to be allowed to be the same as everyone else while also being different from everyone else, and Apion rightly refused.* The reasons for these attacks against the Jews were not irrational or imaginary or trivial, and the label "anti-Semitism" does not help us understand them.

Anachronism and retrojection can be avoided by the substitution of the term "anti-Judaism" for "anti-Semitism," but the essential historical problem centers not on nomenclature but on definition. Even in modern times we often have difficulty in justifying the application of the epithet "anti-Semitic" to a specific incident or text. Some Jews are very sensitive and immediately denounce as "anti-Semitic" any criticism of Israel or any action detrimental to Jewish interests. Other Jews have a much higher threshold and bestow the epithet "anti-Semitic" on only the most blatant and extreme manifestations of anti-Jewish or anti-Israeli behavior. The uncertainty that is at the heart of this contemporary debate has even greater force in our attempted interpretations of anti-Jewish actions and statements from a period in which there was no clearly articulated ideology of "anti-Semitism." Where is that elusive point that separates justifiable hatred from unjustifiable, legitimate opposition from illegitimate, and the "anti-Jewish" from the "anti-Semitic"? To illustrate this uncertainty, let us return to Apion and Hadrian. The former had good reason to dislike the Jews and to oppose their attempts to

---

* If it be objected that I am following the "anti-Semitic" interpretation of the events in Alexandria, I believe that the reconstruction is correct no matter what its origin. For a recent discussion of the issue, see Aryeh Kasher, *The Jews of Hellenistic-Roman Egypt* (Hebrew edition, Tel Aviv, 1978; English edition, Tübingen, 1985) with my review in the *Jewish Quarterly Review* 72 (1982): 330–331.

Shaye J. D. Cohen

obtain civic equality, and the latter had good reason to suppress a Jewish rebellion and to forbid the practices of Judaism. But would Apion's policies have led to the creation of a Jewish ghetto, the profanation of Jewish synagogues, the looting of Jewish property, and anti-Jewish pogroms, had these policies not been motivated, at least in part, by hatred of Jews and Judaism? Would Hadrian's suppression of a rebellion have led to a three-year-long persecution of Judaism and the deaths of numerous martyrs had it not been motivated, at least in part, by hatred of Jews and Judaism? I indicated in the previous paragraph that the simple application of the term "anti-Semitic" to these incidents is neither justifiable nor helpful; but here, I concede, perhaps we must allow for a certain degree of "anti-Semitic" feelings to account for the scale and severity of the incidents. Both Apion and Hadrian crossed the point that separates the justifiable from the unjustifiable, but the precise location of this point is as elusive for historians of antiquity as it is for students of contemporary "anti-Semitism."

A narrow focus on "anti-Judaism" does not do justice to the complexities of Jewish life in antiquity and merely perpetuates the myth that Jewish history is primarily a history of persecutions and martyrs. The Greco-Roman world consisted of those who hated Judaism, those who were indifferent to it, and those who loved it. The latter group included those who embraced Judaism wholeheartedly ("proselytes," or "converts") and those who accepted one or another of Judaism's rituals and beliefs ("God-fearers"). Judaism's denial of the pagan gods and refusal to be incorporated into the religious system of the civilized world (beliefs that could be called "Jewish anti-paganism") aroused both hatred and admiration. A discussion of "anti-Judaism" in antiquity that ignores the other half of the question, the power of attraction exerted by Judaism on the Greco-Roman world, is lachrymose indeed.

Medieval Anti-Semitism

Robert Chazan

It is tedious and usually unnecessary to begin papers with a definition of terms. In this case, however, preliminary delineation of topic is unavoidable. The term "anti-Semitism" means many things to many people, and useful understanding can be achieved only when aspects of this multi-faceted phenomenon are carefully isolated and analyzed. The accepted usages of the term "anti-Semitism" range from the narrow (opposition to and denigration of the Jews as a racial group) to the very broad (any anti-Jewish behavior or attitude). In this paper the term will be used in an intermediate fashion, neither excessively narrow nor excessively broad, focusing on popular negative views and stereotypes of the Jews. The term "medieval" requires less attention, although it too is regularly used in a variety of ways. Again for the purpose of isolating a limited and analyzable aspect of the broader phenomenon of medieval anti-Semitism, this paper will be confined arbitrarily to the newly emerging Ashkenazic communities of northern Europe during the period between 1000 and 1500 C.E. This arbitrary choice on the one hand reflects my own personal interests and expertise; at the same time, the popular anti-Jewish stereotypes that developed in this area during this period are of enormous significance for the overall study of the history of anti-Semitism. In particular, this area forms the major conduit through which earlier anti-Jewish attitudes were funneled into modern Western civilization. Indeed, the imagery of a conduit funneling earlier attitudes is misleading. In northern Europe during the period under discussion, earlier anti-Jewish perceptions were reshaped and refashioned out of the complex interaction of a prior ideational legacy, a specific political-social-economic-religious context, and the realities of Jewish life. The resultant stereotypes constitute a major new anti-Jewish legacy bequeathed by medieval Europe to the modern West; they are therefore fully deserving of careful scrutiny and analysis.[1]

I have defined as my topic medieval (i.e., northern-European, 1000–1500 C.E.) popular perceptions of Jews and Judaism. It must be noted immediately that almost no first-hand statements of these popular prejudices have survived. The literary and artistic materials that remain are all the products of the Christian upper classes and the Jews, presenting what these upper-class Christians and Jews perceived as popular anti-Jewish prejudices. The limitations of the sources must of course be borne in mind; however, this paper is based on the hypothesis that these sources do not massively distort the popular views that they purport to reflect. What I have said already involves an important assumption worthy of explicit articulation. I am assuming that, although there may be recurring themes in the history of anti-Semitism (and I shall deal with some of these), anti-Semitism is not a constant that simply expresses itself in modified patterns from era to era and from area to area. I assume, to the contrary, that the particular constellations of a given majority society, the living patterns of a specific Jewish minority, and usually an inherited legacy of stereotypes combine to create ever-changing manifestations of anti-Jewish thinking and behavior. Indeed, even when an area like northern Europe is examined over a five-century span, substantial change in perceptions of the Jews should be anticipated and in fact is encountered. The focus of this paper will be the shifting pattern of anti-Jewish perceptions in medieval northern Europe

Robert Chazan

and the new legacy thereby engendered and ultimately transmitted to modern Western civilization.

Any effort to depict popular anti-Jewish views and their evolution should properly begin with a broad sense of the larger society in whose context the Jews lived. The basic characteristic of the majority society within which Ashkenazic Jewry emerged was its rapid growth and development. Long a backward hinterland to the more fully developed Mediterranean basin, northern Europe began its precipitous climb to pre-eminence in Western civilization during the second half of the tenth century and in the eleventh century. The foundation for this impressive spurt lay in a material vitalization that included population growth, enhanced agricultural output, industrial invigoration, and the expansion of trade. It was precisely this material progress that made Jewish immigration attractive to some of the most far-sighted political authorities of the area and that made this newly developing region attractive to far-sighted Jews. A concomitant of this general economic efflorescence was accelerated urbanization. In an area where towns had never been large, old urban centers began to expand and new cities emerged. The debate as to whether these urban nuclei developed initially for security, for trade, or as political centers is irrelevant to this discussion. What is important is that they did emerge and did afford an urban base for the Jews coming to settle in this developing region. A third significant characteristic of late tenth- and eleventh-century northern Europe is its enhanced political security and sophistication. The political foundations of this nascent society lay in the direct feudal bond between overlord and vassal. This rather primitive relationship showed the capacity for substantial refinement and sophistication, however, and by the late eleventh century increasingly secure states had been constructed on the basis of the original feudal bond.[2] It was into this political order that the anomalous Jews had to be fit, and feudal society did in fact prove sufficiently supple to accommodate this somewhat unusual group.

The aforecited characteristics of late tenth- and eleventh-century Europe were by and large positive. There were, however, other features of this impressive development that boded ill for the Jews—and sometimes for others as well. One of these negative features was the inevitable violence that afflicted such a rapidly evolving civilization. This was the violence often associated with newness and with tumultuous societal change. Aggression and lawlessness extended from the highest levels of society down through the lowest and posed a profound threat to a small and vulnerable group like the Jews. A peculiar brand of psychological insecurity also plagued this young civilization, especially as its horizons expanded and its awareness of a larger world around it deepened. By the end of the eleventh century, there was already substantial knowledge of this larger world and a concomitant fear of it. Paradoxically, the stronger the new society became, the deeper was its fear of external and internal threats. In addition, the growing sense of identity and cohesiveness in northern Europe—a positive development for most inhabitants of the area—had negative implications for the Jews as relative newcomers and social and religious outsiders.

Into this dynamically developing milieu immigrant Jews were attracted and small but active Jewish urban enclaves were created. It is important to note the major features of these Jewish communities. These Jews tended to live from the outset physically apart—a result of the inclinations of the majority host culture and of the Jewish minority as well. They were generally quite restricted in their economic outlets, by and large confining themselves to trade. Social relations with non-Jewish neighbors were limited. It would be misleading, however, to see these small Jewish settlements as hermetically sealed off from their environment. The towns of the late tenth and the eleventh centuries and the Jewish communities housed within them were simply too minuscule to permit that kind of distancing. Jews spoke the vernacular, were deeply enmeshed in the expanding economy, and absorbed much of the spirit of this vital civilization. The

Jewish social situation was a complex combination of proximity and distance—difficult to comprehend fully and likely to engender complications.[3]

Another element in our background description is the ideational legacy with which this Christian society was equipped or—perhaps better—encumbered. There was one major legacy only as regards the Jews, and that was the traditional heritage of the Catholic Church. In brief, it was a well-worked-out tradition, with elements both positive and negative in constant tension with one another. To begin with the negative, Jews were viewed, on the very simplest level, as religiously wrong. Since a basic Christian assumption was the exclusive religious truth of Christianity, it followed that Jews, along with all other non-Christians, were in error, and indeed the Jews themselves would have said precisely the same of Christians. Because there were no other significant groupings of non-Christians on the European scene, this notion was more problematic than it would have been in a more heterogeneous setting. The Christian negation of Judaism went far beyond this simple rejection, however. Christianity, as a result of its complex evolution out of a Jewish matrix, shared the Jews' sacred literature and claimed proper understanding of the message embodied therein, insisting that the Jews themselves had failed in their comprehension of divine revelation. Thus the Jews were really in a unique category. Unlike all other non-Christians, they had been vouchsafed the truth, misread it, and thereby lost all claims to it. In evaluative terms, the Jews might thus be seen as a notch above all other non-Christians (for they had once possessed the truth) or a notch below (for they had squandered this priceless blessing). Finally, the Jews were alleged to have done worse than reject the messianic figure whom they should have recognized as promised to them—they had done him to death. This was much more than a theological assertion, to be relegated to the limited confines of learned discourse. This was a central element in the major drama of the Christian calendar and liturgy. The celebration of resurrection each Easter Sunday wakened afresh in the most vivid terms the sense of Jewish enmity and malevolence.

All that we have depicted thus far is negative and damning. Taken alone, it should have led to efforts at extirpation of a group so error-ridden and hostile. Against all this, however, was ranged a counter-doctrine, which asserted the right of the Jews to lead a tolerated, albeit limited, existence in Christendom. The rationales for this toleration need not detain us. Suffice it to indicate that they generally involved a negative depiction of the Jews. The result nonetheless was a doctrine of limited toleration. The pious and not-so-pious Christian of the Middle Ages was thus heir to a complex legacy that demanded a stance of toleration toward the Jews, while strongly asserting their ongoing error and hostility. It is not altogether surprising that, under intense pressure, this complex doctrine occasionally unraveled, giving way to over-simplifications and distortions. The inherent complexity of the doctrine invited such unraveling.

This, then, is the background portrait with which we begin: a vigorously expanding northern-European civilization, with problems; a small and dynamic Jewish community, operating under significant limitations; a complex ideational legacy, with a discernible potential for disastrous distortion. It might well be anticipated that, at periods of internal stress and crisis, this potential for distortion might recurrently be actualized.

The first such period came early in the eleventh century. The anti-Jewish incidents are reflected but obscurely in the sources, and I hesitate to present a picture of these events drawn with unwarranted certainty and confidence. It is widely recognized that, at this juncture, the emergent society of northern Europe was confronted for the first time with serious manifestations of internal dissent. This early dissidence was pale in comparison with that which would develop subsequently, but it was alarming and frightening to the establishment and to large segments of the population. A number of disparate sources inform us of anti-Jewish incidents at the end of the first decade of the century and at the beginning of the second decade. In a prior study, I have suggested that these persecutions be understood in the context of the emergence of dissent and its repression. The threat of internal heresy stretched the inherently fragile Church doctrine concerning the Jews to what was for some, both in the establishment and in the populace, its breaking point. Concern with the enemy within Christian circles translated into a parallel fear of the non-Christian enemy living intimately within the confines of European Christendom. It is in this context that the purported mission of Jacob b. Yekutiel to the pope is to be understood. Threatened with death at the hands of the duke of Normandy, Jacob asserted that the propriety of this new policy could be vindicated only by the head of the Catholic Church. Sent on to Rome, Jacob allegedly succeeded in eliciting from the pope a statement of protection strikingly parallel to the twelfth-century *Constitutio pro Judeis,* widely sought by the Jews and recurrently granted by medieval pontiffs. For our purposes, the important point is that internal stress in northern Europe threatened the fragile fabric of toleration of the Jews. The doctrine was strongly reasserted, but the dangers are clear.[4]

The same potential for destructive disintegration of the traditional Church doctrine of negation and toleration—but on a far larger scale—accompanied the exhilarating call to a new-style enterprise of pious aggression in 1095. The papacy, sensitive to newly developing piety and militance, channeled these powerful impulses into a grand military venture against segments of the Muslim world. The vision of the crusade enunciated by Pope Urban II surely projected no overt anti-Jewish implications; most of the crusading armies that coalesced, both professional and popular, managed to gird themselves for war against the Muslims who held the sacred sites of the Holy Land without being stirred to violence against the Jews. In Germany, however, some of the late-developing fervor broke the tenuous complex of negation and toleration, resulting in the notion that a long and arduous journey to do battle against the distant foe should properly be preceded by elimination of the internal enemy, particularly since this internal enemy is ultimately more hostile and reprehensible than the distant one. This is a clear reflection of new-style anti-Jewish thinking that drew its sustenance from the rich prior legacy of Christian anti-Jewish animus and from the social realities of majority and minority status in eleventh-century northern Europe. The sources make it clear, it seems to me, that the limited but devastating crusader assaults on the major Rhineland Jewish communities—Worms, Mainz, and Cologne—cannot be seen simply as incidental popular violence, aimed at plunder of the Jews. These thorough attacks were assimilated by the German crusading bands into the very core of their mission—a distorted ideology, but an ideology nonetheless. The purpose of these assaults was to eliminate entirely the Jews—preferably by conversion or, failing that, by slaughter. Fortunately for Ashkenazic Jewry, this radical distortion of traditional Church doctrine was not widespread, and the bulk of this young Jewry survived the critical spring months of 1096 frightened but unscathed.[5] In the wake of this dangerous propensity for distortion, Church leadership, when evoking a second major crusade in the 1140s, went to great lengths to reiterate traditional doctrine, to identify the crusading distortion, and to repudiate it. Echoes of this distortion can, however, be recurrently discerned in the popular crusading movements that evaded ecclesiastical leadership and control. Popular campaigns against an external enemy quite often aroused hostility against the Jews living within Western Christendom. Perception of the Jew as outsider and enemy must surely be seen as a decisive element in popular medieval anti-Jewish imagery.

The twelfth century brought significant shifts in rapidly evolving northern Europe. A number of these must be identified for the purposes of this discussion. In the first place, the material achievements of the eleventh century were accelerated in every domain—agriculture, industry, and commerce. A special set of circumstances transformed Jewish economic activity in a direction at once useful, profitable, and problematic. At the same time that business was accelerating, an invigorated Church was attacking a series of major abuses, including the sin of Christian taking usury from Christian. This paradoxical combination—enhanced need for capital and an ecclesiastical assault on Christian usury—served to open to the Jews vast new opportunities in banking. Particularly in the more advanced western sectors of northern Europe, England and France, the old alliance between the ruling class and their Jews was intensified by a *de facto* partnership in moneylending, with the Jews supplying the capital and the business acumen and the authorities enforcing the Jewish loans. Both of these developments—the shift in Jewish business specialization and the deepening alliance with the authorities—were for the moment positive. Each, however, added significant negative stereotypes to the primary image of the Jew as enemy. When Bernard of Clairvaux could, in passing and gratuitously, use the verb "to Jew" as a synonym for moneylending, then surely a dangerous new negative image had developed.

There were important twelfth-century developments on the spiritual plane as well. Perhaps most noteworthy is a further broadening of horizons, imparting the sense on the one hand of a vast and interrelated Christian world—a source of pride and strength—and on the other of a large and menacing non-Christian world—evoking fear and insecurity. The same expanding horizons are seen with respect to the microcosm of the individual human soul, with new perceptions of man's nobility and capacity for good and, at the same time, a new awareness of destructive urges and the capacity for evil. This heightened imaginative sensitivity plays a significant, albeit shadowy, role in the shifting perceptions of the Jews. On the popular level, images of the Jews as theologically and socially hostile take the form of a set of slanders that depict them as pathologically spiteful and cruel. The infamous incident at Norwich in 1144 is the first known case of the ritual-murder allegation. When the mutilated corpse of a Christian youngster was discovered outside the town, some of the townspeople immediately imagined the local Jews to be responsible. It should be emphasized that many townspeople disagreed and that the responsible authorities protected their Jews assiduously. Nonetheless, a shrine was established, miracles were claimed, and a local monk penned a detailed and frightful depiction of Jewish cruelty, although he acknowledged freely that no Christian eyes had witnessed the purported event. This is another important development in popular negative imagery concerning the Jews. Hostile theological stereotypes and social tensions are here augmented by new perceptions that identify the Jews as pathologically malevolent and cruel.[6]

The thirteenth century witnessed continued progress in all directions, particularly in the more westerly areas of France and England. The economy grew sounder yet; large and powerful states coalesced; the Catholic Church reached organizational heights undreamed of before; intellectual and artistic creations of impressive scope were spawned; heightened spirituality broke forth in movements both normative and dissident. The sense of external threat remained prominent and engendered continued insecurity and vigilance; the sense of internal threat intensified, leading to bloody repression of those perceived as heretics.

I will first focus on the positive developments and discuss their implications for Ashkenazic Jewry. The first development of major significance was the maturation of government and its ability to control more effectively the society that it ruled. By the end of the twelfth century, the English monarchy had established a system of supervision of Jewish lending that was remarkably comprehensive, and during the thirteenth century France made efforts along the same lines. On one level this was a boon to the Jews—larger sums could be lent with almost absolute assurance of repayment, and indeed the loan instruments were so trusted that they themselves became objects of commerce. From another perspective, however, these developments were problematic. Never before had the Ashkenazic Jews been so clearly and fully under the control of their overlords. Jewish taxes were sufficiently meaningful that the authorities demanded guarantees that their Jews would remain fixed in their pattern of settlement. It seems increasingly clear that the notion of Jewish serfdom, at least in the western areas of France and England, is related to the desire of overlords to fix the residential patterns of their Jews in order to be assured of the tax revenues that these Jews would produce. More damaging yet was the fact that these revenues were so utterly at the mercy and whim of the overlords. No longer was there any mystery associated with Jewish resources and the capacity to pay taxes. In England, at any given moment the authorities could close down the lending centers, study the documentation, assess Jewish wealth, and levy what seemed to be an appropriate tax. Herein lay deep danger. Further Jewish prosperity and profitability depended ultimately on maintenance of a fine balance between ongoing governmental profit and retention of sufficient capital to keep the lending business flourishing. The extent to which these Jews fell under governmental control destroyed that fine balance. The temptation to exploit the essentially defenseless Jews beyond the fine line was simply too great. In England and, to a lesser extent, in France Jewish business was exploited to the point of decline. In all of this the Jewish image had to suffer. Jews inevitably came to be seen as weak pawns of the authorities. Indeed, they became the immediate targets of hostilities that might better have been directed at those who, behind the scenes, manipulated them. In this period, as in all eras, it was far more appealing to vent anger and aggression against the weak than against the strong.[7]

There was a second great danger associated with the maturation of the thirteenth century. As a concomitant of the Church's growth and development, ecclesiastical policy vis-à-vis the Jews reached a new level of articulation and radicalism. Never before had the Catholic Church so clearly defined its stance on all issues, the Jews included. Although this carefully articulated policy was thoroughly grounded in the prior legacy of ecclesiastical legislation, old themes and concerns were stretched in new directions. Three major elements in the Church's demand for intensified limitation of Europe's Jews merit consideration here. The first involved the old issue of potential religious damage through social contact. Church legislation had long aimed at thwarting such damage, but never had the Church pressed so far as to demand that Jews dress in a way that would make them readily distinguishable from their Christian neighbors. This demand, first voiced at the Fourth Lateran Council of 1215, represents a new level in the age-old drive toward social segregation of the Jews and accords well with the tenor of the times. The second intensified thrust of Church legislation had to do with potential Jewish social abuses and with the new reality of Jewish moneylending. The old notion of toleration of the Jews so long as they do not prove harmful took a new twist. The Church now sought to limit what it saw as abuses related to and stemming from Jewish moneylending, demanding that only a reasonable interest rate be charged, that landed Christian debtors not be forced to sell off family property in order to meet their obligations, and that impecunious Christian borrowers not be jailed for failure to pay their debts. All this reflected the broad goal of minimizing Jewish economic and social harm to Christian society. The third element in the Church's new drive to limit potential Jewish harmfulness related to the danger of religious abuse. The Church had long harbored the suspicion that Jews blasphemed against Christianity and its symbols. Now, however, for the first time, the Church became directly familiar with post-biblical Jewish literature and, with this new familiarity, the suspicion became certainty. Out of the inevitable horror at anti-Christian materials in Jewish literature came programs of elimination of the Talmud or, at least, of censoring out offensive sections of the rabbinic tradition. All this is again to be seen as part of the broader thrust of more zealous policing of the tolerated Jews.

It is not surprising that all of these developments should have affected formal secular and ecclesiastical visions of the Jews. For both state and church, the notion of Jewish serfdom gained greater currency and was subjected to more formal definition.

Indeed, Jeremy Cohen has suggested that in some ecclesiastical circles the essential toleration of the Jews was questioned if not abrogated, based on the argument that the talmudic Judaism that had been uncovered during the thirteenth century constituted a deviation from the biblical Judaism that had been the object of Christendom's original grant of toleration.[8] All of this attests to a marked decline in the image of the Jews as reflected in higher levels of society. Little wonder that such a decline should be manifest as well throughout the lower echelons of northern-European society. Notions of Jewish enmity, seen already during the eleventh and twelfth centuries, took on yet more intense forms and became increasingly irrational.

During the thirteenth century, two new slanders made their appearance. Although both were rooted in the traditional Christian view of the Jews as deicides, they represent a new depth of anti-Jewish popular perception. The first—and more lasting—of these popular stereotypes is the blood libel. It in all likelihood proceeded out of the ritual-murder allegation. The temporal scene is once again the Easter-Passover season, with emphasis shifting to the Jewish Passover observance. It is claimed that, as part of their holiday ritual, the Jews ritually imbibe wine made of the blood of slain Christian youngsters. To be sure, the notion of Jewish murder of Christian youngsters developed earlier and the notion of pathological ingestion of murdered children is encountered in the twelfth- and thirteenth-century anti-heretical propaganda. The combination, however, was a potent one and had lasting appeal to segments of the Christian populace, in a way that perhaps investigation of the psychological foundations of folk beliefs will one day elucidate. What is clear is that the Jews were appalled and terrified, turned for assistance to major authorities in both church and state, and elicited decisive repudiation of this irrational allegation. It is equally obvious, however, that rational repudiation did not filter down into the strata of society in which the charge was spawned and where it continued to be nurtured down into the twentieth century. The second new allegation of the thirteenth century likewise revolved around the Easter-Passover season, retaining the original connection with Easter. This slander claimed that the Jews contrived to gain possession of host wafers, usually by exploiting the leverage accruing from unpaid debts. With the wafer in their possession, the Jews then allegedly proceeded to mutilate and torture the transubstantiated body of Jesus, in a compulsive repetition of their original cruelty toward him. Again the irrationality of the accusation—it assumed a Jewish acceptance of the notoriously problematic doctrine of transubstantiation—hardly impeded its acceptance as a widely held popular belief.

There are further indications of increasingly irrational perceptions of the Jews, particularly from the domain of medieval art, which has not yet been studied with sufficient comprehensiveness and rigor for its reflections of anti-Jewish stereotypes. The exploratory studies undertaken thus far indicate a growing tendency toward dehumanization of the Jews, a dehumanization that proceeds in two directions—animalization and demonization.[9] In a sense such dehumanization is an understandable extension of the perceptions of the Jews thus far encountered. With a growing conviction of the absolute rationality of Christianity, those who know it and fail to accept it surely raise questions as to their fundamental capacity for human understanding; a people that possessed the truth and gave it up—indeed, that still possesses and studies the literature in which this truth is embodied without properly understanding it—raises serious doubts as to its mentality; a people that could condemn its promised messiah to death, that could reenact this act of cruel malevolence recurrently, and that could do so in ways inhumanly malicious would hardly seem to qualify as part of the human species. Again a focus on the Jews and the issue of anti-Semitism should not blind the historian to the fact that other groups suffered similar stigmatization. For many reasons, however, the Jews were a primary target of such dehumanization. One form taken was a tendency to depict the Jews in animal-like fashion. The recent exhaustive

Robert Chazan

study by Isaiah Shachar of the *Judensau* motif affords striking illustration of the tendency and, at the same time, a methodological model for further research.[10] A second avenue for dehumanizing tendencies was demonization, the imputation of intimate links between the Jews and the omnipresent satanic forces at work in the world. The notion of an allegiance between the Jews and the devil is of course older, but the linkage gained greater acceptance and force during the thirteenth century.[11]

With the end of the thirteenth century came an end also to Jewish presence in the more advanced western areas of northern Europe. Ashkenazic Jewry was relegated to the central and eastern sectors of northern Europe, which tended to be less well developed economically, politically, and spiritually. It was the lack of economic development that made the Jewish presence useful and viable; on the other hand, political immaturity made the area violence-prone and therefore insecure for the Jews; the lack of spiritual and intellectual advancement preserved and fostered the damaging negative stereotypes that had already been produced in this northern-European milieu.

In sum, northern-European society, caught up in a process of rapid growth and development, attracted Jews and directed them into economic avenues that were useful, profitable, and problematic. Out of its own tensions, the constricted realities of Jewish life, and an earlier legacy of anti-Jewish stereotypes, this budding civilization spun out a series of increasingly irrational and damaging fantasies regarding its Jews. Eventually, the more advanced sector of this civilization excluded these Jews, pushing them eastward into areas less advanced and still needy. In such areas, the anti-Jewish stereotypes of the eleventh through the thirteenth centuries embedded themselves tenaciously. Even in those regions from which the Jews had been expelled, the anti-Jewish imagery continued its own independent existence. Thus, as European civilization entered a dynamic new phase of growth and development from the sixteenth through the eighteenth centuries, in the process reopening to Jewish settlement areas long closed, a powerful anti-Jewish legacy pervaded the entire culture. With the emergence of revolutionary new ideas regarding the organization of the state and relations between ecclesiastical and secular authorities, many—in both the Christian majority and the Jewish minority—felt that the death knell had sounded for the anti-Jewish images so obviously rooted in classical Christian thinking. These optimistic observers failed to reckon, however, with the tenacity of such stereotypes and the suppleness with which they could be adapted to new circumstances, both material and spiritual. Most students of modern European anti-Semitism discern behind nineteenth- and twentieth-century rhetoric the disastrous imagery created during the first epoch of Ashkenazic Jewry's development on European soil.[12]

NOTES

1. In addition to popular imagery, there are ecclesiastical, governmental, and scholarly views of the Jews. These views, of course, impinge on the popular imagery and vice versa. Again, for the purposes of careful analysis this discussion will arbitrarily focus on the popular imagery.

2. This impressive development is depicted in Georges Duby, *The Early Growth of the European Economy,* trans. Howard B. Clarke (Ithaca, 1974); Marc Bloch, *Feudal Society,* trans. L. A. Manyon (Chicago, 1961); R. W. Southern, *The Making of the Middle Ages* (London, 1953).

3. The fullest study of this early Ashkenazic Jewry is that of Irving A. Agus, *The Heroic Age of Franco-German Jewry* (New York, 1969). Also useful is the general depiction of Jacob Katz, *Exclusiveness and Tolerance* (Oxford, 1961), pp. 3–63.

4. I have analyzed these incidents more fully in "1007–1012: Initial Crisis for Northern-European Jewry," *Proceedings of the American Academy for Jewish Research* 38–39 (1970–1971): 101–117.

5. I have analyzed the impact of the First Crusade on northern-European Jewry far more fully in my forthcoming *European Jewry and the First Crusade.*

6. The major source is the lengthy account of Theobald of Monmouth, published and translated by August Jessopp and Montagu James, *The Life and Miracles of St. William of Norwich* (Cambridge, 1896).

7. This view of the development of Jewish serfdom in the western areas of northern Europe can be found in my *Medieval Jewry in Northern France* (Baltimore, 1973) and in Gavin I. Langmuir, "Tanquam Servi: The

Change in Jewish Status in French Law about 1200," *in* Myriam Yardeni, ed., *Les Juifs dans l'histoire de France* (Leiden, 1980), pp. 24–54.

8. Jeremy Cohen, *The Friars and the Jews: The Evolution of Medieval Anti-Judaism* (Ithaca, 1982).

9. Note the pioneering studies of Bernhard Blumenkranz, especially his *Le Juif Médiéval au Miroir de l'Art Chrétien* (Paris, 1966).

10. Isaiah Shachar, *The Judensau: A Medieval Anti-Jewish Motif and Its History* (London, 1974).

11. See Joshua Trachtenberg, *The Devil and the Jews* (New Haven, 1943) for much of the material on this important theme. Further analytic work remains to be done in this area.

12. This is argued with special vigor by Jacob Katz in his *From Prejudice to Destruction: Anti-Semitism, 1700–1933* (Cambridge, Mass., 1980).

Robert Chazan's "Medieval Anti-Semitism":
A Note on the Impact of Theology

Jeremy Cohen

Robert Chazan has presented a succinct tripartite model to explain the etiology and character of medieval anti-Semitism. His thesis is "that [1] the particular constellations of a given majority society, [2] the living patterns of a specific Jewish minority, and [3] usually an inherited legacy of stereotypes combine[d] to create ever-changing manifestations of anti-Jewish thinking and behavior." This formulation presents an approach to medieval Jewish history that recognizes that anti-Semitism was never a simple phenomenon; it derived from a multitude of interdependent components of medieval civilization. And should such an impression sound truistic it can hardly be overstated, given the great number of writers who have attempted to account for Christian anti-Judaism in the Middle Ages from a narrow, parochial standpoint—whether that of the social, economic, political, or cultural historian. It is hoped that such a broad and balanced perspective will provide the basis for a fruitful revisionist inspection of all extant evidence of medieval anti-Judaism, an undertaking in which Professor Chazan has already begun to play a leading role.

This is not the appropriate place for me to attempt any such review of specific historical events, but I would like to reflect briefly on several of the issues raised in this insightful synthesis. First, although Professor Chazan has confined his attention to

Ashkenazic Jewry, one cannot overlook the Iberian contributions to the development of anti-Semitism. As a crossroads of Jewish, Christian, and Muslim civilizations, medieval Spain occupied an admittedly unique station in the history of medieval Europe; it therefore defies generalization. Yet the anti-Jewish legislation of the Catholic Visigoths, the singular phenomenon of Marranism, and the zealous persecutions of the Spanish Inquisition all testify to a hatred of Jews that even conversion to Christianity failed to mitigate—exceptional for the Middle Ages, to be sure, but a significant precedent for the racial anti-Semitism of the nineteenth and twentieth centuries.

On a more general note, Professor Chazan has defined his subject as the legacy of medieval anti-Semitism in the *Weltanschauung* of modern Western civilization—the popular anti-Jewish stereotypes of the European Middle Ages insofar as they ultimately contributed to more recent Gentile perceptions of the Jew. From such a developmental perspective, I would incline to argue that the ideational component in his explanatory model warrants greater emphasis than that allotted to it. I grant that the precise time, place, and intensity of an instance of medieval anti-Semitism resulted directly from the particular characteristics of the Gentile and Jewish communities involved in the interaction. With the possible, partial exception of the stereotypical usurer, however, I believe that the substance—that is, the accusations, the beliefs, the value judgments—of most medieval anti-Jewish expression derived from the teachings of Christian theology above all else. Theology afforded the encounter between medieval Jew and Gentile its uniqueness. No other period in our history knew such an extensive rule of a single religious establishment, especially one in whose overall world view the Jews and Judaism figured so importantly. A few examples should illustrate my point. From the earliest generations of the Catholic Church, Christian clergymen deemed it a religious duty to polemicize against the Jews. Where the latter posed little or no immediate threat to the Church, or even in the complete absence of Jews, the *Adversus Judaeos* tradition continued to flourish; for the logic of early Christian history dictated the affirmation of Christianity in terms of the negation of Judaism. In a word, the specific theological assumptions of the two faiths were mutually exclusive. As John Chrysostom, one of the most revered fathers of the Church, instructed his parish in fourth-century Antioch:

> Where Christ-killers gather, the cross is ridiculed, God blasphemed, the father unacknowledged, the son insulted, the grace of the Spirit rejected. . . . If the Jewish rites are holy and venerable, our way of life must be false. But if our way is true, as indeed it is, theirs is fraudulent. I am not speaking of the Scriptures. Far from it! For they lead one to Christ. I am speaking of their present impiety and madness.[1]

As a result, the theme of the negation of Judaism permeates the literature of classical Christian theology. And the continued existence of the Jews in a Christian world demanded theoretical justification, usually in the notion that the Jews still somehow served God's purposes—in their preservation of Scriptures, which prefigured the New Testament; in their properly enforced wretched state of physical dispersion, which bespoke their true character; and in their expected future conversion to Christianity. Yet this idea of a wandering Jew who was a pawn in God's plan for the salvation of the Gentiles, which entailed the belief that God steered the course of Jewish history to demonstrate the truth of Christianity, boded ill for the Jews—both in medieval and in modern times. "Stated with theological finesse," Richard Rubenstein concludes, in recounting his discussions of the Nazi Holocaust with Christian clergymen in post-war Germany, "it comes to pretty much the same thing as the vulgar thought that the Christ-killers got what was coming to them."[2] The epithet of "Christ-killer" is itself illuminating in this regard. Modern Jews and Christians—even the Second Vatican Council—too frequently have viewed the Jewish role in Jesus' trial and crucifixion, along with charges of such involvement, as a mathematical problem. Surely some Jews participated, but surely not all did. How many, then? A few? Most? We often fail to consider that the New Testament description of the Jew as Christ-killer is theological categorization, not even a highly biased account of what actually happened, and that this theological category irreversibly colored the medieval Christian idea of the Jew.

With respect to the relation between elite and popular perceptions of the Jews in medieval Christendom, I would agree with Professor Chazan that we can and must accept the reflections of popular views in the extant literary and artistic sources as reasonably accurate. But I would also submit that we ought not to underrate the anti-Judaism of the medieval Christian leadership—at times viewed profitably as distinct from the evolving popular approach to the Jews. Or, to put it a bit differently, theological subtlety also contributed in its own right to the anti-Semitic legacy of the Middle Ages. Again, one or two examples should suffice.

In an essay entitled "The Medieval Conception of the Jew," Cecil Roth describes the late medieval idea of the Jew as deliberate unbeliever, one who embodied the most satanic and unnatural proclivities imaginable; the Jew knew the truth of Christianity and spitefully spurned it anyway—hence the license with which he (allegedly) recklessly killed, poisoned, tortured, and blasphemed within Christian society.[3] But Roth and others after him did not realize that prior to any popular expression of this idea of the Jew, Christian professors of theology at the University of Paris formulated a new interpretation of the New Testament verses that alluded to the Jews' deicide. Previously the prevalent opinion held that the Jews had killed Jesus in ignorance of his divine and messianic character. Beginning in the thirteenth century, Christian biblical commentators taught that the Jews recognized Jesus as their savior and son of God but killed him deliberately nonetheless. It is true that the blood libel took the idea of deliberate unbeliever further than the theologians intended; however, its theoretical, academic roots still ought not to be forgotten.

Jeremy Cohen

Furthermore, one ought to recall that from the first century onward, the Christian attitude toward the Jews remained inextricably intertwined with the Church's estimation of Jewish books; popular Christian anti-Judaism, therefore, may never be disjoined from the tendencies of the literate clergy, who also stereotyped in a grand way. During the early Middle Ages, Christians valued the Jews because of their Scripture, whose primary meaning the Church considered its Christological one. Real Jews were simply assumed to be the fossils of antiquity that a Christian reading of Scripture necessitated; as Beryl Smalley has aptly put it, "Philo's 'wise architect' [of allegorical exegesis inherited by the early Church fathers] had built a prison for the Jewish people." [4] By the twelfth century, churchmen had recognized that the Hebrew Bible did have a prior literal meaning that preceded that of Christian allegory; Jews were then valued even more for their learning, because they offered the most direct link to the historical context of ancient biblical Israel. Such a development itself proved theologically problematic, however: How could the Jews understand Scripture better than Christians if as biblical religions Judaism and Christianity were mutually exclusive? Some thirteenth-century academicians attempted to resolve the problem by affirming the literal sense of Scripture but denying that Jews still understood it. And if contemporary Judaism no longer embodied the religion of the Old Testament, what rightful place had it in Christendom? Only in the thirteenth century did the Church begin to burn Jewish books and did Latin churchmen begin to advocate the exclusion of the Jews from a properly ordered Christian society.

My variations on Professor Chazan's picture of medieval anti-Judaism reaffirm my appreciation of the value of his analysis. To enlighten successfully, any model must stimulate serious question and discussion. When all is said and done, I myself believe that Professor Chazan's depiction of this phenomenon will remain substantially intact.

NOTES

1. Homily 1, *Against the Jews,* trans. in Wayne A. Meeks and Robert L. Wilken, *Jews and Christians in Antioch in the First Four Centuries of the Common Era,* Society for Biblical Literature, Sources for Biblical Study 13 (Missoula, Mont., 1978), p. 97.

2. Richard Rubenstein, *After Auschwitz: Radical Theology and Contemporary Judaism* (Indianapolis, 1966), p. 56.

3. Cecil Roth, "The Medieval Conception of the Jew," in *Essays and Studies in Memory of Linda R. Miller,* ed. Israel Davidson (New York, 1938), pp. 171–190.

4. Beryl Smalley, *The Study of the Bible in the Middle Ages,* 2nd ed. (Notre Dame, 1964), p. 26.

Jeremy Cohen

Anti-Semitism and the Muslim World

Jane S. Gerber

The study of anti-Semitism in the Muslim world is more than a definitional and semantic exercise. It is a study in theology and politics and their unique amalgam in time and space. Jews and Muslims have coexisted continuously since the birth of Islam, sometimes symbiotically and at other times antagonistically. Their interaction has been on such a wide historic canvas and in such a variety of circumstances that any generalization about the status of the Jews will be schematic at best. Even during its era of greatest unity (ca. 800–1200) the Islamic empire was not one historical entity but rather a dynamic human reality composed of a mélange of different languages, people, cultures, and regimes. Disparities in time, attitude, and general cultural level characterize the Jews under Islam so palpably that comparison even within the Muslim orbit is extremely difficult.

By juxtaposing the situation of the Jews in smoothly functioning, pluralistic, sixteenth-century Ottoman society[1] and the virtual caste system of rigidly stratified nineteenth-century Yemen,[2] or the exuberant Jewish life of Fatimid Egypt and the degradation of nineteenth-century Cairene Jewry,[3] the historian is confounded. Although the same theoretical framework regarding Jews prevailed in the courts and bazaars of fourteenth- and eighteenth-century Morocco, the quality of Jewish life in the two instances differed markedly.[4] Indeed, so varied is the historical experience of Jews in Muslim lands that virtually any thesis, be it negative or positive, can be buttressed by historical evidence.

Analyses of anti-Semitism in Muslim lands are often flawed by the misleading analogy or comparison with the European Jewish experience. In general, Jewish life in Muslim lands was characterized by persistent discrimination and degradation. In Europe, on the other hand, Jewish life was prey to violent persecutions, not local episodic depredations, and crushing discriminatory legislation. The institutionalized and frequently systematic anti-Jewish discrimination confronted by European Jewry through the ages stands in marked contrast to the smooth flow of life of Jews under Islam. Although the Prophet Muhammed spoke of the Jews of his day in copious detail, the place of the Jew was entirely different in the Muslim *Weltanschauung* from the Christian one. Moreover, the gap between theory and practice, between anti-Jewish ideology and anti-Jewish behavior, was always wide in the lands of Islam.

Anti-Semitism in the Muslim world must be studied *sui generis*. Comparisons with Europe have led either to an unwarranted idealization of the Islamic past and its treatment of minorities or to an equally unscientific tendency to view all anti-Jewish manifestations, both Eastern and Western, as part of a universal pattern of tribulations in exile, undifferentiated by regime, law, time, or place. This latter tendency is undoubtedly strengthened by the habit of Jewish chroniclers—in both Europe and the Muslim world—of depicting Jewish tribulations stereotypically as *gezerot, pera 'ot,* or *tzarot hatzorer.*[5] As a result, the reader is left with an impression of Jewish life in the Diaspora as uniformly and eternally plagued by the irrational, unpredictable, and all-encompassing evil of anti-Semitism.

Any systematic and nuanced study of anti-Semitism in Muslim lands must also take into account the divergent attitudes held by various populations in the Muslim world. Although obvious, this factor should nonetheless be stated, because Western stu-

Jane S. Gerber

dents are frequently unfamiliar with the decentralized, fragmented, and unstable nature of Islamic history. Sunni Muslims and Shi'ite Muslims, Malikis and Shafi'ites within the Sunni branch of Islam held varying views of Jews, which prevail until today. Sectarians and fundamentalist revivalists did not hesitate to exploit popular negative sentiments regarding the position of the Jews as a platform upon which they would seize power.[6] Even the Shi'ites did not manifest a uniform attitude toward Jews. Whereas tolerance toward Jews was a basic part of the statecraft of the sectarian Fatimids in medieval Egypt, Zeidis in Yemen displayed none of this tolerance. Varieties of outlook toward Jews in Muslim lands were also influenced by the diverse positions of the Christian minorities toward Jews. This is especially the case in the early modern era when Christian anti-Semitism, rather than Muslim intolerance *per se,* embittered Jewish existence. Yet commonalities do exist, and the diverse strands or population groupings among Muslims ultimately draw upon a common legacy regarding Jews. This legacy reaches back to the dawn of Islam in Arabia and the paradigm of the Prophet Muhammed.

Consideration of the Jewish condition and of the attitudes toward Jews in Muslim lands is best achieved through a division of Islamic history into four main parts for purposes of analysis. The era of Muhammed and the expansion and consolidation of the conquests, from approximately 620 to 800, forms the core of our subject. The second historical division of Muslim-Jewish relations extends from approximately 850 to 1200 and includes the age of Muslim imperial grandeur. During this epoch, frequently called "the intermediate period" or the age of the "bourgeois revolution" and the "renaissance of Islam," Jewish communities proliferated and Jewish life flourished in the major cities of Spain, North Africa, and the Near East.[7] Even during this era of cooperation, creativity, and intellectual cross-fertilization, Muslims believed Jewish existence to be inferior or subordinate. The third period of Muslim-Jewish relations coincides with the fragmentation of the various Muslim empires, a brief period of Ottoman ascendancy in the sixteenth century, and an extended period of decline lasting until the introduction of Western imperialism and European cultural influences around 1800. This triggered the emergence of a new set of power relationships and mutual perceptions between Muslims and non-Muslims.[8] The fourth and latest period in the development of anti-Semitism in Muslim lands is the so-called modern era, a highly volatile period of partial modernization in Middle Eastern societies during which European notions and modes of anti-Semitism have been increasingly domesticated in the Muslim world. Although the advent of Zionism and the Arab-Israeli conflict have exacerbated Muslim-Jewish relations, the emergent anti-Semitic doctrine has been heavily dependent upon traditional Islamic precepts, returning today almost full cycle to the first period of the Muslim-Jewish encounter.

Each of the four aforementioned periods can, of course, be further refined. The evolution of anti-Semitic theory in the modern era, for example, can be roughly divided into three periods, 1917 to 1948, 1948 to 1967, and 1967 to today. The earlier eras are also internally divisible. Yet, given the centrality of Islam in the past as well as in modern Arab ideologies, it is the first period of Islamic history that forms the heart of all discussions of Muslim anti-Semitism.

The life of Muhammed, the sayings of Muhammed preserved by traditionalists in the Koran and the *hadith,* and the practices ascribed to Muhammed by loyal followers and later legal compilers form a distinct body of attitudes and directives regarding the Jewish people. These layers of Muslim tradition are considered by Muslims to be either divinely revealed (as in the case of the Koran) or divinely inspired and hence of eternal relevance and applicability. For the Muslim believer, the great drama of Islam unfolds on a single stage, and the various layers of his tradition are not subject to scientific modes of examination to determine authenticity or partial validity. The Western notions of modern criticism of Scripture are entirely alien or highly problematic at

Jane S. Gerber

best to even the most liberal Muslim theologians. It is not accidental that Muhammed's attitudes toward Jews, Judaism, and Israel were the subject of an international conference convened at the Azhar in Cairo in 1968, drawing together the most distinguished theologians from every corner of the Muslim world and producing a major, multi-volume compendium of Muslim anti-Semitism.[9] Clearly, contemporary Muslims of the highest rank continue to draw inspiration from historic confrontations embedded in the earliest stratum of Islamic history.

It used to be said that Islam emerged in the full light of history. Today it is increasingly clear that the gaps in our knowledge concerning the life of Muhammed are enormous and that there are as many theories about the life of the Prophet as there are biographers. Scholars disagree on the extent to which Muhammed's message was dependent upon the Jews. However, all recognize that the core of his revelation is embedded in day-to-day tribulations in Mecca and Medina and the critical role played by Jews in the Medinese phase of the new religion's advent. Acting as both spiritual guide and secular leader after his emigration from Mecca to Medina in 622 (the *Hijra*), Muhammed encountered the opposition of approximately twenty-odd Jewish clans and three major Jewish tribal groupings in Medina, forcefully meeting the challenge of their resistance to his message in that oasis commercial center. Koranic echoes of Muhammed's disputes with the Jews enable us to see the emergence of a complex and essentially ambivalent attitude toward Jews on Muhammed's part. This ambivalence has been incorporated into the literature and teachings of Islam *vis-à-vis* Jews.

Islamic ambivalence regarding Jews derives from the earliest history of Islam, a religion that did not seek to sever its ties with Judaism completely. Initially Muhammed appears not to have seen any distinction between his notions and those of the Jews and was taken aback by Jewish opposition to his claims of Prophetic finality and perfection. The Koran preserves some of the Prophet's polemics with Jews as lively verbal exchanges, verbal jousts, and biting or sarcastic polemics; these later gave way to refutations and condemnations. The Koran recognizes the ethnic kinship and cultural affinities between Jews and Muslims; nevertheless, it also preserves treaties between Muhammed and the Jews that clearly enunciate the Muslim view of political and religious superiority. Jews are not asked to become Muslim in these treaties, but to pay tribute and to submit to Muslim supremacy. Possibly such an arrangement derived from Arabian custom, whereby a strong tribe would take a weak tribe under its protection.[10]

Precedents regarding the Prophet's treatment of the Jews varied: Where politically expedient and militarily feasible, Muhammed did not hestitate in expelling two of the Jewish tribes from Medina. His extermination of the third main tribe, the Qurayza, was also recorded in the Holy Scriptures of Islam. By and large, Muhammed was a consummate politician, able to live with groups that did not threaten his supremacy. He drew a distinction between the Jews as descendants of Abraham, recipients of a partial revelation with whom he was willing to contract treaties, and the Jews as an ignoble people possessed of a rebellious and malevolent spirit who were corrupters and obscurers (*tahrif*) of Scripture.[11]

Although Muhammed branded the Jews as enemies of Islam, he did not go so far as to outlaw them or to remove them entirely from Arabia. Instead, the Koran distinguishes between warfare with pagans, which was to be total and relentless, and with Jews and Christians. The Koran is laced with anti-Jewish pronouncements. In Sura 3:63 Jews are labeled "corrupters of Scripture," and in 3:71 they are accused of falsehood. In Sura 4:46 Jews are condemned for their distortion, and Sura 5:85 declares, "Thou wilt surely find that the strongest in enmity against those who believe are the Jews and the idolaters." The theme of Jewish hostility toward Muslims is reflected in the eighth-century *hadith*, "A Jew will not be found alone with a Muslim without plotting to kill him."[12] Cowardice, greed, and chicanery are but a few of the

Jane S. Gerber

characteristics ascribed to the Jews by Muhammed, who asserted that they were accursed by God and metamorphosed into apes.

For the Muslim the Koran holds special authority. It is the literal word of God as mediated to Muhammed through the angel Gabriel. Koranic phrases are prefixed by the expression "God has said"; the phrase "the Prophet said" is used in traditions ascribed to Muhammed. According to the teaching of Muhammed, the religion preached by all the prophets is essentially one and the same, although there is a gradual evolution toward the final and perfect faith of Islam. Muhammed cites four God-given Scriptures, the Tawrah (Torah), revealed to Moses; the Zabur (identified with the Psalms), given to David; the Injil (Gospels), given to Jesus; and the Koran. All are written revelations, all are valid, and all are to be believed. The Koran, however, as the last revelation, clarifies all uncertainties left in the minds of believers by prior revelations.

Muhammed's theory of prophecy complements his view of successive revelations. The religion of Judaism derived from the laws of Moses and Christianity from the teachings of Jesus; Muhammed went behind both historical personalities to the figure of Abraham. According to Islam, Abraham, being neither Christian nor Jew, was the progenitor of a pristine, undistorted monotheism that was constantly revived by successive prophets. In this manner Muhammed kept himself within a historic continuum while setting himself apart from his predecessors.[13] Muhammed's theory of prophecy contained within it the seeds of disparagement of Jews and Judaism, but it also served a preservative function. According to an early *hadith* Muhammed is reported to have said, "He who harms a member of the protected nation—I shall be his prosecutor on the Day of Judgment."[14]

According to classical Islamic theory the possessors of Scripture, *Ahl al-Kitab* (literally, People of the Book), were to be combatted until they were subdued and agreed to pay tribute. Critical to any discussion of anti-Semitism in the Muslim world is this concept of toleration. According to the Koran the Muslim believer is exhorted (Sura 9:29), "Fight against such as those who have been given the Scripture and believe not in Allah nor in the Last Day, and forbid not that which Allah hath forbidden by his messenger and follow not the religion of truth, until they pay the tribute readily, being brought low." Some translations have the alternative reading "until they humbly pay tribute out of hand." This central Koranic verse embodies the dual notion of tribute bearing and humiliation as the price of toleration.

From the earliest days of Islam the *dhimmi* status of Jews and Christians (as well as Zoroastrians) guaranteed these groups the right to practice their religion. The abasement of Jews decreed in the Koran became proof of divine decrees of the "proper" place of the Jew in Muslim lands. In the emerging empire of Islam and the hierarchical structure of the Middle East, the Jew's distinctive and inferior status was shared with other groups. The radical isolation of the Jew as "outsider" in Europe was never approximated in the Muslim world. Still, the notion of toleration-protection *cum* humiliation took varied, frequently ingenious, and sometimes outrageous forms. Ludicrous clothing, mismatched shoes, prohibitions against going outdoors in the rain, and a variety of other discriminatory laws set the Jew off as a *dhimmi* at various times in different Muslim countries.[15] Jews were objects of officially legislated contempt, but they were not intended to be objects of officially instituted hatred.

Tolerance of Jews and Christians was incorporated into a system of separation, subordination, and fiscal tribulation quite early in Islamic history. Certainly by the reign of the eighth-century Caliph 'Umar II, the main contours of a system of discrimination were articulated.[16] The rendering of special payments for protection (*djizya*) was only one part of a complex relationship of superiority of Muslim and inferiority of Jew. The *dhimma* system emerges as part of a tight legal system and the end product of the systematizing of jurists during the Abbasid period. Significant for the prehistory of this system is the document commonly known as the "Constitution of Medina," wherein the

Jane S. Gerber

status of the Jews in Medina is fixed by the Prophet as that of a separate *Umma,* or community (if religion is the main criterion of *Umma*), or as part of the general *Umma* of Medina while the separate religion of Judaism is retained. Three times in the Koran *Ahl al-Kitab* (the People of the Book) and *Ahl ad-Dhimma* (Protected People) are linked.[17] Ultimately Koranic traditions, local usage, *ad hoc* arrangements, and informal agreements on specific disabilities were systematized and were collectively known as the Pact of 'Umar, being ascribed retroactively to the early pious Caliph 'Umar I.

The step-by-step crystallization of humiliating measures for *dhimmis* served to reinforce the initial Koranic assumption of inequality of Jew and Muslim. The restrictions flowing from the general presumption of Jewish inferiority were extremely varied, ranging from special dress as a "mark of distinguishing" (*ghiyar*) or "mark of recognition" (*shi'ar*) to humiliating status symbols (such as donkey riding) and limitations on social and professional mobility. As a rule, the dress regulations were spasmodically implemented and had to be renewed periodically. They appear to have been more regularly operative on the fringes of the Muslim world, in such countries as Iran, Yemen, and Morocco, and were more widespread in application in later centuries than in earlier periods.[18] It should be recalled, however, that in return for adherence to these signs and symbols of inferiority the Jews received the precious and virtually unqualified right of freedom of conscience and worship in a modest manner.

Muhammed's vitriolic attack upon the Jews that peppers the pages of the Koran, combined with its implied system of protection and inequality, has profoundly affected the Muslim. Not only is Muhammed's conduct worthy of unquestioning emulation in Muslim society, but also the very notion of the past is perceived differently. Until today, preoccupation with the Muslim past, particularly its medieval and more heroic chapters, consumes more than one half the scholarly efforts of the Muslim world and plays a pronounced role among the masses.[19] By perceiving the past as inextricably woven into the present—as a living phenomenon competing, as it were, with the present—the Muslim is continually influenced by the theological threads of anti-Semitism embedded in the earliest chapters of Islamic history. This might explain the ease with which that legacy has been superimposed upon the Arab-Israeli conflict and how even contemporary battles in the Sinai or on Golan have been transformed into earlier confrontations of Muhammed and his foes.[20]

What are the positive features of this formative period that should be emphasized? Although it is difficult to laud a system of discrimination and contempt that must surely be considered anathema by contemporary standards, it nevertheless should be clear that the Muslims devised a formula for religious pluralism in which the Jews could survive and even prosper. Despite the fact that their lives were worth less than a Muslim's from the point of view of Islamic criminal law and their civil and political rights were limited, they could enjoy the fruits of the expansive age of Islamic expansion from the ninth through the twelfth century.[21] Jewish settlement in those centuries was widespread, continuous, and almost unbroken within the strictures set by the founders and formulators of Islam.

The founder of Islam instituted a system marked by hostility, discrimination and degradation vis-à-vis the Jews, yet the historian is confronted by an apparent contradiction. How are we to understand the long period of creativity and prosperity that the Jewish community enjoyed in Muslim lands between the ninth and the twelfth centuries? Do the brilliant careers of Spanish and Iraqi Jews in the courts and salons of caliphs and princes not belie the entire system of discrimination formulated by Prophet and jurist? Are they refutations of the theory of *dhimmi* status, emphasized by scholars ineluctably drawn into the polemics of the contemporary Middle East? To what degree was Muslim anti-Semitism attenuated by the fact that Jews under Islam, unlike their coreligionists in the Christian world, were not the only group deemed inferior? Haven't the Muslim modernists eschewed the more archaic notions of pristine Islam in any case? None of these questions is rhetorical; they ask whether the theory of Jewish inferiority was merely a theory or was based to a significant degree in fact.

Jewish life in the second period of Islamic history is most elaborately documented in great richness and detail, largely because of the availability of Geniza records and the monumental scholarship of Professor S. D. Goitein in reconstructing medieval Jewish society in the Mediterranean world. A disproportionate amount of material is available to analyze this period, compared with the earliest period of Islam and the late Middle Ages. With the consolidation of the Muslim conquests and the end of the long and bloody feuds between Byzantines and Persians, the Mediterranean world entered an era of economic expansion, intellectual curiosity and cultural borrowing, personal mobility and population growth. Just as Jews suffer to an acute degree the pangs of a sick society, so too they enjoy to a well-known degree the fruits of an era of economic expansion, political optimism, and relative stability. The conquests of Islam restored to circulation great accumulated riches that had been frozen in private possession, created new cities and new classes with a taste for luxury, stimulated the emergence of new industries such as the textile industry, and generally favored urban expansion. Whether the discriminatory legislation regarding the Jews was applied consistently or with severity depended upon the whims of local rulers and the volatile masses. In general, political or military reverses or tensions with the Christian world would exacerbate Muslim-Jewish relations and ignite anti-Jewish sentiments. In addition, flagrant violation of the *dhimmi* status, such as through the conspicuous exercise of political power by a Jew, would provide fodder for a religious reformer, who would incite the wrath of the masses and demand that discriminatory legislation be re-instituted.

Whereas the proscription of Judaism and Christianity by the twelfth-century Almohades is exceptional and the attacks on Egyptian Jewry by the eccentric Fatimid al-Hakim are singular, the historic examples of the fate of the Ibn Nagrela family in Spain and Haroun el-Battas in fifteenth-century Fez are instructive. The diatribes against the Jews of Spain by Ibn Hazm and Abu Ishaq are characteristic expressions of a civilization that took the message of Jewish degradation quite seriously. Those who overstepped the bounds of Jewish humiliation were perceived to have broken the contract of protection through arrogance and haughtiness, and death was their just punishment. The emergence of a Jewish courtier in a position of power should not be interpreted as a sign that the system of discrimination was merely theoretical but rather should be understood as a symptom of a situation in which the ruling authorities did not possess the requisite tribal or military base to consolidate their rule and were consequently forced to rely upon Jews.

A balanced view of the period of greatest Muslim-Jewish cooperation (850–1200 C.E.) should distinguish between the very real Jewish intellectual advances and economic diversity and the ephemeral and precarious Jewish approximations of civil or political power. Ultimately, all Jewish attempts at approximations of a position of political equality were deemed to be unlawful and provocative violations of the spirit of the Pact of ʿUmar, even in the era of greatest Islamic stability and tranquillity. Should the Jew enjoy his wealth too conspicuously or diverge from his position of *dhull* (humiliation and abasement), he could not expect that the original relationship of contractual protection would necessarily be honored.[22]

Although it is true that a psychological difference exists in being the sole pariah (as was the Jew's case in the Christian world) or being a scorned group in an empire in which other groups were also scorned, the documentation provided by travelers to the Muslim world suggests that not all *dhimmis* were treated equally, in the sense of being equally scorned! The Jews appear to have been the lowest *dhimmis* for many centuries, even within the Islamic system of legislated discrimination. This fact is particularly applicable to the Ottoman period, when the European powers

Jane S. Gerber

began to extend a protective hand to various Christian groups within the Muslim world. The eighteenth-century Damascus barber Ahmad al-Budayri, for example, describes a week-long festival given by a Damascus Muslim notable to which all classes and social groupings were invited each day, in descending order, according to social status. The Jews outranked only the peasants and prostitutes.[23] Even visitors to Morocco in the same era who were unsympathetic to Jews deplored their wretched status.[24]

By 1800 the position of the Jews in Muslim lands was precarious in the extreme. The perceptive European observer Edward W. Lane, visiting Cairo in the 1830s, noted in his *Manners and Customs of the Modern Egyptians* that "the Jews of Egypt are under a less oppressive government in Egypt than in any other country of the Turkish Empire." Still, he observed:

> Not long ago, they used to be jostled in the streets of Cairo, and sometimes beaten merely for passing on the right hand of a Muslim. At present, they are less oppressed: but still they scarcely ever dare to utter a word of abuse when reviled or beaten unjustly by the meanest Arab or Turk; for many a Jew has been put to death upon a false and malicious accusation of uttering disrespectful words against the Koran or the Prophet. It is common to hear an Arab abuse his jaded ass, and, after applying to him various opprobrious epithets, end by calling the beast a Jew.[25]

During the period of the Qajar dynasty in Iran, a very difficult era for all Iranian Jews, a European described the bitter humiliation of Jews as follows:

> At every public festival—even at the royal salaam before the King's face—the Jews are collected, and a number of them are flung into the *hauz* or tank, that King and mob may be amused by seeing them crawl out half-drowned and covered with mud. The same kindly ceremony is witnessed whenever a provincial governor holds high festival: there are fireworks and Jews.[26]

An interesting confirmation that the *dhimmis* were not given equivalent treatment comes from the testimony of Turkish officialdom in its description of the Christian response to the promulgation of the *Ḥatti Ḥumayun* of 1856. The decree proclaimed the equality of Muslim and non-Muslim in the Ottoman Empire. Cevdet Pasha, a high Turkish official, noted the consternation of Ottoman Christians:

> As for the non-Muslims, this day, when they left the status of *raya* and gained equality with the ruling *millet,* was a day of rejoicing. But the patriarchs and spiritual chiefs were displeased, because their appointments were incorporated in the firman. Another point was that whereas in former times, in the Ottoman State, the communities were ranked, with the Muslims first, then the Greeks, then the Armenians, then the Jews, now all of them were put on the same level. Some Greeks objected to this, saying: "The government has put us together with the Jews. We were content with the supremacy of Islam." [27]

This observation introduces another element in the Middle Eastern anti-Semitic equation that has become increasingly significant since the nineteenth century—the role played by the Christian populations in the Muslim world both as economic rivals of the Jews and as repositories of a strong (indeed, virulent) antagonism toward Jews as deicides harking back to at least the fourth century. As the native Christians began to enter the mainstream of Near Eastern national life, they injected a new note into the anti-Semitic refrain. For a variety of reasons that extend beyond the scope of the present study, Christian Arabs have been the most articulate formulators of modern Arab nationalism. In the process of articulating this nationalism they have been deeply influenced by Western notions, including classical Western anti-Semitic formulations regarding the Jews. [28]

The Ottoman period does not provide a particularly illuminating historic stage on which to view the playing out of Muslim anti-Semitic doctrines. Instances of murder, extortion, humiliation, and degradation were the order of the day for all peoples within its disintegrating society. The final period of anti-Semitic development in the Muslim world, the modern era, is perhaps the most difficult to discuss. From the early nineteenth-century Western incursions, the impact of the West has proved to be a destabilizing influence in all areas of life. Not only has the Muslim self-confidence in the invincibility of Islam been shattered by the spectacle and the experience of Western imperial domination, but also the advent and success of Zionism has provided an additional element of mass trauma to an already overheated and xenophobic nationalist scene. The modern period has been characterized by an outpouring of anti-Semitic literature that frequently bears strong resemblance to medieval European Christian polemics or Nazi-style diatribes in its vulgarized demonization of the Jews.

It is difficult to ascertain the precise relationship of this new voluminous body of literature to the older Muslim doctrines regarding Jews. A process can be discerned within an evolving situation. Today anti-Jewish expressions from the Koran and early Muslim writings are lifted out of context and grafted onto contemporary discussions and situations. As this is done, the formerly ambivalent traditional image of the Jew in the Muslim mind has become progressively more sinister.

One of the startling new elements in Muslim anti-Semitism that is clearly attributable to Christian influence is the motif of the blood libel. As the Western powers extended their influence in the Middle East through missionaries, educators, military missions, and bankers, the anti-Semitic baggage of the Christian intellectual tradition was appropriated by Muslims. Foremost among Christian notions was the infamous blood libel. Initiated by Near Eastern Christians, the blood libel was easily accepted by many Muslims. Instances in Aleppo (1811, 1853), Beirut (1824), Antioch (1826), Hamma (1829), Tripoli (1834), Dayr al-Qamar (1847), and Damanhur (1877) and the infamous Damascus blood libel of 1840 (followed by further libels in Damascus in 1848 and

1890) are not fully representative of the frequency with which this contagious calumny occurred. What is of significance is the ease with which this foreign libel was integrated into the traditional Muslim view of the Jews. The *ḥadith* of the Jew plotting to kill the Muslim as well as the Koranic motif of the Jew as the enemy of Muslims and mankind (Sura 5:85) have been invoked by more than one leading Muslim theologian in recent years. The prooftext frequently invoked to prove these spurious charges against the Jews is none other than the *Protocols of the Elders of Zion!* A contemporary Cairo historian, Abd al-Karim Gharayiba, wrote of the Damascus blood libel that "the mothers would caution their children not to go out alone late at night, lest the Jew Abu Al-'Afia would come and take their blood for the purpose of making *matzot* for Passover."[29] The motif is vividly embellished and transformed in contemporary literary depictions of Israelis and Jews and amply analyzed by such Israeli scholars as Harkabi and Sivan. It is therefore hardly surprising that the late King Feisal should reiterate the motif in the most widely read Arabic weekly *al-Musawwar:*

> Israel has had malicious intentions since ancient times. Its objective is the destruction of all other religions. It is proven from history that they are the ones who ignited the Crusades at the time of Saladin the Ayyubid so that that war would lead to the weakening of both Muslims and Christians. They regard the other religions as lower than their own and other peoples as inferior to their level. And on the subject of vengeance—they have a certain day on which they mix the blood of non-Jews into their bread and eat it. It happened that two years ago, while I was in Paris on a visit, the police discovered five murdered children. Their blood had been drained and it turned out that some Jews had murdered them in order to take their blood and mix it with the bread that they eat on this day. This shows you what is the extent of their hatred and malice toward non-Jewish peoples.[30]

Though not one of the stock images of Jews in traditional Islamic society, the blood libel has been "domesticated"; it has been linked to more familiar images of Jewish enmity toward Muhammed and Islam. Through the widespread use of media and textbooks this new anti-Semitism has become rooted.

Since 1948, and especially since 1967, the line between anti-Zionism and anti-Semitism has become increasingly blurred in both serious literature and the popular press in the Muslim world. An ominous new note of dehumanization and demonization of the Jew can be discerned in the anti-Israeli vocabulary of Arab leaders who compare Israel with a bacillus, plague, or cancer. Although the translation of the *Protocols of the Elders of Zion,* which has appeared in numerous editions, and the Arabic version of Drumont's *La France Juive* have been labeled as foreign literature, one cannot help questioning whether these translations can be considered foreign any longer after fifty years of currency in the Arabic language and multiple editions.

A final element that must be isolated in the most recent phase of anti-Semitism in Muslim lands is the recurring theological refrain. Despite the wide gap separating the fulminations of Muhammed in seventh-century Medina that God will bring humiliation upon the Jews,[31] the medieval Maghrebi *fetwas* prohibiting Jewish physicians from donning the attire of a Muslim gentleman,[32] and President Sadat's famous speech of April 25, 1972 promising to crush Israel and return it to "the humiliation and wretchedness established in the Koran," a thread of continuity runs through Islamic history. There has been no courageous theological breakthrough that would limit or possibly abolish the ancient notions of discrimination. Instead, Islamic reform as espoused by such great thinkers as Muhammed Abduh and Islamic fundamentalism as represented by such groups as the Muslim Brethren have urged Muslims to "rethink Islam" and return to the sources. Reformers of both liberal and reactionary proclivities have tended to extoll certain virtues and values of Muslim tradition that strengthen the sentiment of Islamic supremacy.[33]

The fate of the Jews in Muslim lands has been different from that of their European co-religionists through the ages largely because Muslim anti-Semitic notions and theories have been different from those of Europeans. Prior to the emergence of the anti-Semitism of the modern era, survival of Jews (albeit frequently in a position of abject servility) could be reasonably assured. Such an assertion cannot be made today with any degree of certainty as Koranic notions and Western anti-Semitic currents form new strains of thought in Muslim lands.

Living in an age of unusual and unprecedented persecution in the Islamic world, Maimonides lamented in his *Epistle to Yemen:*

> And you, my brethren, know that on account of our many sins, God hurled us amidst this nation of hostile Ishmael. . . . Never has a nation risen more injurious to us than this people; no nation has ever been so intent on humiliating us and degrading us. That is why when David, king of Israel, was shown in an inspired vision all the tribulations which were to overwhelm Israel, he did not cry out, or ask for help for our people, until he saw what we were to suffer in the kingdom of Ishmael; and then he exclaimed, 'Woe is me that I sojourn in Mesech, that I dwell in the tents of Kedar!' [Ps. 120:5].[34]

Historical knowledge enables the modern student of anti-Semitism to realize that the tents of Kedar were not as forbidding as they appeared from the vantage point of twelfth-century crisis that marked the age of Maimonides; nor were they nearly as hospitable as modern legend or apologetic propaganda would like us to believe. The balance lies somewhere in between.

NOTES

1. Benjamin Braude and Bernard Lewis, eds., *Christians and Jews in the Ottoman Empire,* 2 vols. (New York, 1982).
2. Yosef Tobi, "Ha-merkazim ha-Yehudiyyim be-Asya" in Y. Tobi, Y. Barnai, and S. Bar-Asher, eds., *Toldot ha-Yehudim be-Artzot ha-Islam* (Jerusalem, 1981).

Jane S. Gerber

3. The most extensive description of medieval Jewry in Egypt can be found in S. D. Goitein, *A Mediterranean Society,* 4 vols. (Los Angeles, 1968 to 1983). See Edward William Lane's description in *The Manners and Customs of The Modern Egyptians* (London, 1954), pp. 558–562.

4. Jane S. Gerber, *Jewish Society in Fez 1450–1700* (Leiden, 1980), chapter 1.

5. A typical example of this form of historical writing is *Divrei ha-Yamim le-Yehudei Morocco,* by Saadia Ibn Danan, et al. (library of the Jewish Theological Seminary of America manuscript collection).

6. Gerber, op. cit., p. 19, and *Kisse ha-Melakhim* by Raphael Moses el-Baz, Sassoon Collection, manuscript no. 1064, p. 22.

7. Adam Mez, *The Renaissance of Islam* (London, 1937). See S. D. Goitein, "The Unity of the Mediterranean World in the 'Middle' Middle Ages," *Studia Islamica* 12 (1960): 29–42, for a discussion of periodization.

8. See later discussion. Also Sylvia M. Haim, "Arabic Anti-Semitic Literature: Some Preliminary Notes," *Jewish Social Studies* 17 (1955): 307–312, and Norman A. Stillman, "New Attitudes Toward the Jew in the Arab World," *Jewish Social Studies* 37 (1975): 197–204.

9. D. F. Green, ed., *Arab Theologians on Jews and Israel* (Geneva, 1974).

10. Tor Andrae, *Mohammed: The Man and his Faith* (New York, 1960), and Montgomery Watt, *Muhammad, Prophet and Statesman* (Oxford, 1961), p. 193. On the possible Bedouin precedent, see Claude Cahen, "Dhimma," *Encyclopedia of Islam,* new edition (Leiden, 1960–1978).

11. *Koran* 3:63; 3:71; 4:46, 160–161; 5:41–44, 63–64, 82; 6:92 and passim.

12. Quoted by Samuel Rosenblatt, "The Jews and Islam," in Koppel S. Pinson, ed., *Essays on Anti-Semitism* (New York, 1942).

13. Hamilton A. R. Gibb, *Mohammedanism* (New York, 1958), p. 31. Some scholars feel that the shrines of Mecca already bore some relationship to the stories of Abraham and Ishmael and that this linkage represented an authentic Arabian tradition and not a transparent borrowing from Judaism.

14. Moshe Maoz, "Anti-Jewishness in Official Arab Literature and Communications," in Moshe Davis, ed., *World Jewry and the State of Israel* (New York, 1977), p. 34.

15. Claude Cahen, op. cit.; J. Gerber, "The Pact of 'Umar in North Africa: A Reappraisal of Muslim-Jewish Relations," in *Proceedings of the Seminar on Muslim-Jewish Relations in North Africa* (New York, 1975), pp. 40–51, and Laurence D. Loeb, *The Outcaste: Jewish Life in Southern Iran* (London, 1977), pp. 292–293.

16. Claude Cahen, "Djizya," *Encyclopedia of Islam,* new edition. The taxes were burdensome and collection appears to have been complicated and sometimes humiliating. A. S. Tritton quotes a Muslim saying, "A Jew will never pay his taxes till he has his head smacked," in *The Caliphs and Their Non-Muslim Subjects* (Oxford, 1930), p. 95. The correlation between taxa-

tion and its impact upon conversions to Islam has been noted in particular in Daniel C. Dennett, *Conversion and the Poll Tax in Early Islam* (Cambridge, 1950).

17. *Koran* 2:62; 5:69; 22:17.

18. A few standard studies on the disabilities imposed upon the *dhimmis* exist. In addition to Tritton's 1930 work, op. cit., see Antoine Fattal, *Le Statut Legal des Non-Musulmans en Pays d'Islam* (Beirut, 1958). The full list of anti-Jewish disabilities in Iran is found in the appendix of Laurence D. Loeb's *The Outcaste: Jewish Life in Southern Iran* (n. 15).

19. Bernard Lewis, "Islamic Concepts of Revolution," *Islam in History* (New York, 1973), and E. Sivan, *Modern Arab Historiography of the Crusades* (Tel Aviv, 1973). The sensitive perceptions of Islam by Edward Said confirm some of these Orientalists' observations. Cf. Edward W. Said, *Covering Islam* (New York, 1981).

20. Y. Harkabi, *Arab Attitudes Toward Israel* (New York, 1972); Moshe Maoz, op. cit.

21. Majid Khadduri, *War and Peace in the Law of Islam* (Baltimore, and London, 1955), and "International Law," in M. Khadduri and H. J. Liebesny, eds., *Law in the Middle East* (Washington, 1955).

22. Abu Ishaq, the eleventh-century secretary to the *qadi* of Granada, incited the masses to revolt against the Ibn Nagrelas and their co-religionists precisely on these grounds. By exercising power over Muslims in an allegedly arrogant manner they had revoked the terms of *dhimma* and were deserving of death. See Bernard Lewis, "An Ode Against the Jews," *Islam in History,* op. cit., pp. 158–166, and Moshe Perlmann, "Eleventh-Century Andalusian Authors on the Jews of Granada," in *Proceedings of the American Academy for Jewish Research* 18 (1949): 284–290.

23. Ahmad al-Budayri al-Hallaq, *in* Ahmad Izzat Abd al-Karim, ed., *Ḥawadith Dimashq al-Yawmiyya* (Damascus, 1959), p. 112.

24. Charles de Foucauld, *Reconnaissance au Maroc* (Paris, 1888).

25. Edward W. Lane, *Manners and Customs of the Modern Egyptians* (London, 1954), p. 559.

26. C. J. Wills, *Persia as It Is* (London, 1887), p. 231.

27. Braude and Lewis, op. cit., 1:30.

28. Attacks on the Bible and the Talmud are common in this literature. They are no longer the preserve of Christian authors but have been appropriated by many contemporary Muslims. Jewish "racism" and "malevolence" are traced to biblical and talmudic teachings. See, for example, Ali Abd al-Wahid Wafi, *al-Yahudiyya wa'l-Yahud* (Cairo, 1970), or Mustafa al-Sa'dani, *Adwa' 'ala'l-Sahyuniyya* (Cairo, 1969), and particularly Harkabi's discussion in *Arab Attitudes Toward Israel* (op. cit.), pp. 218–304.

29. Abd al-Karim Gharayiba, *Suriyya fi al-Qarn al-Tasi Ashar 1840–1876 (Syria in the Nineteenth Century)* (Cairo, 1961–1962).

30. Quoted by Norman Stillman, op. cit., p. 197.

31. *Koran* 2:61, 112; 7:152.

32. al-Wansharisi, "La Pierre de Touche des Fetwas de Ahmad al-Wanscharisi," Fr. trans., E. Amar, *Archives Marocaines* 12–13 (1908–1909).

33. For a brief appraisal of the literature of reformist Islam see Pierre Rondot, "Minorities in the Arab Orient Today," in J. Landau, ed., *Man, State and Society in the Contemporary Middle East* (New York, 1972), pp. 271ff., and Albert Hourani, *Arabic Thought in the Liberal Age 1789–1939* (New York, 1962).

34. Moses Maimonides, *Iggeret Teman* (Epistle to Yemen), edited by Abraham S. Halkin and translated by Boaz Cohen (New York, 1952), p. xviii, and Moshe Perlmann, "Eleventh-Century Andalusian Authors on the Jews of Granada," op. cit., p. 290.

Comparative Perspectives on Modern Anti-Semitism in the West

Todd M. Endelman

Historical accounts of the development of anti-Semitic ideas in the modern period make tedious reading regardless of their intellectual merit. The fault rests not so much with the authors—who include some distinguished scholars—as with the materials with which they must contend. Despite the inflammatory character of anti-Semitic writings and their murderous consequences, the intellectual arsenal of anti-Semitism has been relatively impoverished, containing only a very limited number of themes lacking both sophistication and complexity. Reduced to its bare essentials, modern anti-Semitism has rested on a handful of accusations about Jewish character and behavior: Jews are malevolent, aggressive, sinister, self-seeking, avaricious, destructive, socially clannish, spiritually retrograde, physically disagreeable, and sexually overcharged. This brief catalogue of Jewish shortcomings and vices exhausts the ideological battery of anti-Semitism at its most basic level; most anti-Semitic polemic has been little more than a reworking of these themes.

In addition, the same assertions about Jews have cropped up regularly everywhere in the West. In country after country, the same libels and reproaches have been heard in one forum or another. Even in the most liberal states of the West—Great Britain and the United States—where relations between Jews and Gentiles have been amicable on the whole, expressions of vicious racial anti-Semitism have not been absent. As the recent studies of Michael Dobkowski and Colin Holmes make clear,[1] Eastern and Central Europe by no means enjoy a monopoly on vulgar racial anti-Semitism. Thick-lipped, hook-nosed sinister Jews engaging in every species of criminal and sexual knavery have appeared in anti-Jewish pamphlets and cartoons in both liberal and conservative states.

Yet if the same libels about Jews have appeared everywhere in the West, the accents and stresses in anti-Semitic thinking have varied from country to country. Usually, the basic axioms of Jew-hatred were translated into forms appropriate to the national context in which they were expressed. Thus, in early-twentieth-century Germany and Austria, where Jews were prominent in literature, journalism, music, and theater, the so-called judaization of culture was a central theme in the thinking of most anti-Semites. By contrast, fears about Jewish aggression were rarely couched in terms of increasing Jewish domination of the arts in Great Britain, where the role of Jews in cultural life was minimal. There, as in America, accusations about Jewish influence in the economy in general and in banking in particular figured more prominently. Thus, however universally disseminated the fundamental themes of modern anti-Semitism, they were not immune to the impact of national context. Indeed, this impact extended to more than the content of anti-Semitic rhetoric. The larger question of the greater or lesser receptivity of different societies to anti-Semitism in general, a critical matter to which we shall soon return, can be answered only by reference to the national contexts in which anti-Jewish ideas flourished or languished, as the case may be. Tracing the development of these ideas without reference to the ground in which they grew will not illuminate the impact of anti-Semitism in modern history. However, before we pursue this issue, it is necessary to return briefly to the content of anti-Jewish thinking.

At one time historians routinely believed that a major shift

Todd M. Endelman

occurred in anti-Semitic thinking in the 1870s and 1880s.[2] Early anti-Jewish writing, it was argued, was primarily religious in inspiration: The Jews, having rejected and murdered Jesus of Nazareth, were eternally damned, condemned by God to wander the earth as perpetual aliens. Conversion to Christianity, however, could save them from theological damnation and social odium; those who rejected the perverse, blasphemous, stiff-necked ways of Judaism would be rewarded with assimilation into Christian state and society. On the other hand, these historians argue, modern anti-Semitism was fundamentally secular in its assumptions about Jewish malevolence: The stain of Jewishness was rooted in the racial character of the Jew, in his fundamental essence, in his biological make-up, and was thus impervious to the cleansing power of the baptismal font. No matter how strongly they repudiated their traditional customs and beliefs and how ardently they embraced the majority culture, Jews and ex-Jews were no longer welcome in Gentile society.

Recent research, while not denying the genesis of a distinctly political anti-Semitism in the 1870s and 1880s, has tended to downplay the novelty of the racial anti-Semitism that allegedly made its debut at that time and to stress the continuity of anti-Semitic beliefs since the beginnings of Jewish emancipation in the previous century. George Mosse, for example, has convincingly demonstrated that European racism originates in the Enlightenment of the eighteenth century, when "the structure of racial thought was consolidated and determined for the next one and three-quarters centuries."[3] In a similar vein, Leon Poliakov has shown that the myth of the Aryan race was launched by the first decade of the nineteenth century and internationally accepted by the 1860s.[4] At mid-century many educated Europeans believed, explicitly or implicitly, that the racial origins of an individual determined his inner character and genius, that racial characteristics were inheritable and racial groups eternally fixed, and that environmental factors were generally incapable of altering habits of thought and behavior. In regard to German anti-Semitism specifically, Jacob Katz has found abundant evidence of a growing belief in the immutability of Jewish character (and hence its incapacity for assimilation and imperviousness to baptism) as early as the 1790s.[5] To cite only one particularly shocking example: The young Fichte, who believed that the characteristics of the Jews were so rooted in their nature as to be beyond alteration, wrote in 1793 that the only way to grant them citizenship "would be to cut off their heads on the same night in order to replace them with those containing no Jewish ideas."[6]

Clearly, it was possible for practicing Christians in the eighteenth and nineteenth centuries to hold racial views about the character of the Jews, if by "Christian" we mean not the official teachings of the churches but the thoughts and feelings of ordinary flesh-and-blood Christians, most of whom were unconcerned about theological doctrines. Then as now, most persons had no difficulty in accommodating logically incompatible ideas among the stock of notions with which they viewed and judged the world's affairs. Even in much earlier centuries, in early modern Spain and Portugal, there had been theologically sophisticated churchmen who defended the statutes of purity of blood, which barred New Christians (converts from Judaism and their descendants) from important offices and honors, on the grounds that the consequences of Jewish ancestry were indelible, perpetual, and unalterable.[7]

The inability of theology to dislodge prejudice in the Iberian peninsula and later in Central Europe is not difficult to understand if we consider how deeply rooted in the popular imagination were the Church's views about the eternal wickedness and otherness of the Jews. What Yosef Yerushalmi has written about the Iberian experience applies equally well to European society in the last two centuries:

> . . . Christian teaching had harped incessantly upon such enduring Jewish qualities as stubbornness, stiff-neckedness,

obduracy, rigidity. The Jews were depicted, not only as un-
yielding, but as unchanged since the primal sins of their
ancestors. Their physical attributes became stereotyped in
art, folklore and the popular imagination. The whole of
Christian Europe had been conditioned in this way, and this
cannot but have contributed profoundly to mold a mental
conception of the Jews which Christian dogma did not reflect—one of their essential immutability.[8]

The persistent theological degradation of the Jews by the
Church resulted, then, in an altogether unintended consequence:
widespread doubt about the efficacy of Christian sacraments to
save Jewish souls. Moreover, once Christianity had accustomed
men and women to thinking about Jews in a certain way, it
became very difficult to dislodge these familiar patterns of perception even when Christian faith, which had implanted them
initially, began to weaken and, in some regions, crumble. The
rapid decline of the Christian churches in western and Central
Europe in the nineteenth and early twentieth centuries failed to
dilute the strength of anti-Semitism. Whether or not men and
women still attended church or read the Gospels, they continued
to see the Jews in a negative light. The rise of nationalism, with its
emphasis on the organic unity of the national community, encouraged this negative perception by reiterating the alienness
of the Jews. To be sure, the vocabulary of anti-Semitism became secular—accusations of racial mongrelization and capitalist
knavery replaced those of blasphemy and deicide—but the fundamental animus remained constant: The Jew was the embodi-
ment of evil. His image served the same function in the mind of
the modern anti-Semite that it had in the mind of his ancestors: It
represented the forces of darkness that were seeking to over-
whelm the world he knew. In the medieval world, the Jew was
the ally of the Devil and the sworn enemy of Christendom,
poisoning its wells and murdering its children. In recent times,
the Jew was the bearer of those forces transforming and threaten-

ing traditional society—capitalism, liberalism, secularism, urbanization, materialism. In either case, the Jew appeared as malevolent, rapacious, and aggressive.

From these remarks, one might infer that anti-Semitism has been pretty much the same at all times and in all places and that histories of anti-Semitism are clever exercises and not much more. Or, as Sigmund Freud confessed to Arnold Zweig in 1927, "With regard to anti-Semitism, I don't really want to search for explanations; I feel a strong inclination to surrender to my affects in this matter and find myself confirmed in my wholly non-scientific belief that mankind on the average and taken by and large are a wretched lot." [9] In fact, Freud's position is not my own. Thus far I have intentionally restricted myself to a discussion of anti-Semitic *ideas*—rather than parties, legislation, or violence—and have stressed continuity in anti-Semitic thinking and the diffusion of anti-Semitic ideas for a specific reason: to emphasize the limited utility of studying the development of anti-Semitic ideas in isolation from the history of their reception in specific historical settings. [10] For clearly anti-Semitism—in the broadest sense of the term—did not have the same impact everywhere, however widely diffused its basic beliefs. It does not take the professional expertise of a historian to know that it was easier to be a Jew in London than in Berlin.

From this perspective the critical issues in the history of anti-Semitism involve asking how and why anti-Semitic ideas were transformed into social and political realities that disrupted and embittered the lives of Jews. One needs to ask why these ubiquitous anti-Semitic ideas found a mass audience in one country and a limited reception elsewhere. Why did they appeal to some social groups more than others? Why did some groups attempt to translate their hatred and fear of Jews into a system of social and legislative discrimination while others vented their prejudices only at home? In other words, we need to ask what people do with the beliefs and slogans that are available to them. The French grocer who purchased a copy of Eduard Drumont's

La France juive but failed to vote for an anti-Semitic deputy, loot a Jewish shop, insult Jews in the street, or otherwise concretely demonstrate his allegiance to anti-Semitism did not pose the same threat as those of his fellow Frenchmen who did. Similarly, the contemporary American housewife who tells a survey research interviewer that Jews are clannish, dishonest in business, and too powerful in finance and government but does not translate her beliefs into action (for example, by supporting far-right anti-Semitic groups or blackballing Jewish candidates for membership in local organizations) remains a closet anti-Semite, with little impact on the course of Jewish history.[11]

In the years between Napoleon and Hitler, anti-Semitism found expression in a wide variety of ways, ranging in intensity from the trivial to the life-threatening. In most countries, elite social circles excluded *arriviste* Jews eager to acquire the social recognition they thought appropriate to their newly acquired wealth, and in some instances also restricted their entry into exclusive professional and educational institutions. The widespread exclusion of American Jews from metropolitan and country clubs, resorts and hotels, and college fraternities and sororities, and the imposition of quotas by private universities and preparatory schools, especially on the eastern seaboard—discriminatory activity that began in the late 1870s and did not weaken until a century later—represent some of the most well-known attempts to obstruct the social ascent of wealthy Jewish families. More serious, in terms of the numbers affected and the suffering inflicted, were government statutes that restricted the participation of Jews in economic and political life and denied them equal standing before the law. In the German states before 1871 and in the Hapsburg empire before 1867, Jews were routinely prevented from settling in certain towns and entering certain occupations. Even after their formal emancipation, Jews in German-speaking lands still suffered from a persistent pattern of bureaucratic discrimination, which, contrary to law, barred them from the most prestigious offices in those societies—the army, the diplomatic corps, the judiciary, the upper levels of the civil service, and the highest ranks in the university. In addition, in both Germany and Austria political parties and pressure groups arose from the late 1870s on to challenge the newly acquired legal equality of the Jews and seek legislation restricting their participation in public life. Political anti-Semitism of this nature was not characteristic of the West in general, however, but largely confined to Germany, Austria, and, to a lesser extent, France, although during the Great Depression it reared its head most everywhere.

With the great exception of Nazi-dominated Europe, violent attacks on Jewish persons and property, although not altogether absent in western Europe and America during the modern period, never constituted a serious threat to the security of these Jewries, as was the case in earlier periods and contemporaneously in eastern Europe. Of course, it is not difficult to cite instances of organized attacks on Jews in the West—the Hep Hep riots of 1819 in Germany, the riots in Alsace during the revolutions of 1830 and 1848, the activities of the British Union of Fascists in the East End of London in the 1930s, anti-Jewish vandalism by the Christian Front and the Christian Mobilizers in New York City in the late 1930s and 1940s. And, in the case of the United States, where outbreaks of violence were commonplace and urban inter-group conflict rife, anti-Jewish hooliganism was not infrequent in neighborhoods where Jews and members of other ethnic groups lived in close proximity to each other. But in both western Europe and America, anti-Jewish violence was not endemic. Few Jews in the West ever faced—or feared they would face—a frenzied mob shouting anti-Semitic slogans.

Much more unsettling for the Jews of the West, especially those seeking acceptance into Gentile circles, was the pervasive disparagement of Judaism and Jews in literature, on the stage, in journals and newspapers, in speeches and debates, in jokes and cartoons. Unflattering stereotypes that wounded Jewish sensibilities were invoked not only on the political right but also by liberals and moderates, who might have disclaimed any intention to sow hatred of Jews. Charles Dickens, whose villainous Fagin is one of the best known Jewish characters in English literature, naively claimed in 1854, "I know of no reason the Jews can have for regarding me as 'inimical' to them."[12] Dickens's Fagin and thousands of other less skillfully drawn literary and journalistic portraits reinforced the popular notion that Jews were dangerous creatures, up to no good, untrustworthy and unscrupulous. Jews everywhere came in frequent contact with these popular images, and in the last resort the discomfort they inflicted may have done more to encourage the flight from Jewishness than social exclusion and occupational discrimination.

Public denigration of Jewish character was not a novel phenomenon in the nineteenth century; there was nothing peculiarly "modern" about these verbal assaults. What was new was their impact on their intended victims. In prior centuries, when Jews accepted their exclusion from society more willingly, the hostility of the Gentile world was an accepted fact of life. Jews then did not pursue honor and intimacy outside their own community, so Christian contempt was largely irrelevant to their own sense of identity and well-being. But when Jews began moving into new spheres of activity in the age of emancipation, they became acutely sensitive about their public image and thus vulnerable to a new source of discomfort. At the same time, their integration into new areas of activity produced resentment on the part of non-Jews, who vigorously resisted this penetration in many instances. The anti-Semitism surrounding the Dreyfus affair, for example, while employing the hoary myths of Jewish disloyalty and treachery, focused on a radically new phenomenon in European history—the presence of Jews in positions of prestige and power in the very heart of Gentile society. There could have been no parallel to the Dreyfus affair—or, similarly, to the storm over A. Lawrence Lowell's imposition of a quota at Harvard in 1922—at any time before the late nineteenth century.

Among the various expressions of Jew-hatred in the modern

period, some were clearly more threatening than others, and in order to note this I want to introduce a distinction between what I will call public and private forms of anti-Semitism. The former refers to the eruption of anti-Semitism in political life—the injection of anti-Semitism into matters of public policy and the manipulation of anti-Semitism for partisan political ends. Specifically, it describes the activities and beliefs of anti-Semites who sought to harness the coercive power of the state to their hatred and fear of Jews, with the goal of reversing Jewish emancipation by legislative or bureaucratic means and thereby blocking the integration of Jews into the mainstream of national life. Private anti-Semitism refers to expressions of contempt and discrimination outside the realm of public life—in business and industry, in clubs and resorts, in private schools and universities, on the stage and in the press. Private anti-Semitism includes the activities and beliefs of persons and groups who were content to express their dislike for Jews in private acts of contempt and exclusion, without turning to the state—and hence to the political arena.

Of these two broad categories, public anti-Semitism clearly posed the graver threat to Jews, since it sought to mobilize the power of the state against Jewish integration and socioeconomic mobility. Ideological in character, it incorporated an originally unstructured cluster of popular attitudes toward Jews into a critique of contemporary social and cultural problems resulting from the transformation of older values and patterns, and viewed the resolution of the "Jewish Question" as a critical step toward the restoration of national health and prosperity. Whereas anti-Semitism outside the realm of politics tended to be a casual and informal matter, frequently resting on unarticulated and inert assumptions about Jewish character and behavior, public anti-Semitism was a more raucous, strident affair, whose growth depended on the advent of mass literacy and mass politics. The manipulation of public opinion—by means of rallies and marches, posters and petitions, newspaper and journal articles, songs and cartoons—was a key ingredient in public anti-Semitism. Indeed,

Todd M. Endelman

many conservative statesmen who otherwise disliked Jews opposed public anti-Semitism precisely because its spokesmen employed rabble-rousing, crowd-pleasing techniques with the potential of disrupting public order.

Significantly, public and private anti-Semitism were not found in roughly the same proportions everywhere in the West. Public anti-Semitism was noticeably more prevalent in Germany and Austria than in Great Britain and the United States, with France falling somewhere between the two extremes. This pattern was not accidental but the direct outcome of the particular histories of these states. Specifically, the strength of public anti-Semitism everywhere was linked to the vitality of cultural and political anti-modernism. In those states where the fundamental ideas of bourgeois liberalism (religious toleration, parliamentarianism, equality before the law, occupational mobility, laissez-faire capitalism) failed to attract widespread support, e.g., Germany and Austria, there was less willingness to tolerate the integration of Jews than elsewhere. Men and women who endured economic hardship and suffered a loss of social prestige as a result of the rise of industrial society, who resented being pushed to the fringes of the new society and felt overwhelmed by and isolated from it, developed a generalized hostility toward all forces that seemed to weaken traditional economy and society and threaten well-established values and styles. Their disaffection from modern society almost always wore an anti-Semitic face, since Jews were associated with all the destructive forces of modernization—capitalism, urbanization, democratization, materialism, socialism. After all, were not Jews among the chief beneficiaries of the collapse of the *ancien régime?* Had not the progress of liberalism brought about their emancipation and the march of Manchesterism their *embourgeoisement?* It was only a short leap from associating Jews with modernization to holding them responsible for all of its ills. Thus a comprehensive solution to the intractable problems of society was readily available—rid society of Jewish influence. "This was a convenient way of attacking the existing order," Shulamit Volkov has observed, "without demanding its total overthrow and without having to offer a comprehensive alternative." [13]

Anti-modernism was not a uniquely central European phenomenon; it appeared in all industrializing countries of the West during the nineteenth and early twentieth centuries. But only in Germany (and, to a lesser extent, in Austria) did it become a dominant sentiment among broad segments of the population; only there did it eventually determine the outcome of history, as the Nazi years testify. Not uncoincidentally, anti-Semitism played a greater role in public life in Germany than elsewhere in the West. The state and imperial governments systematically excluded Jews from offices and posts of high rank and status; influential right-wing pressure groups, such as the Alldeutscher Verband and the Bund der Landwirte, incorporated anti-Semitism into their public campaigns; the Conservative Party, one of the pillars of the imperial political establishment, openly and explicitly embraced anti-Semitism in 1892, declaring its intention to "combat the widely obtruding and decomposing Jewish influence on our popular life" [14]; newspapers and journals carried a steady stream of articles inveighing against the Jews; in short, public anti-Semitism was respectable in Germany, endorsed by social and political elites clinging tenaciously to preindustrial, feudalistic values; it was a major ingredient in the illiberalism characteristic of so much of German political culture before 1945. [15] "It was," as Peter Gay has written, "part of, and clue to, the larger question: the German Question." [16] No other western country had a "Jewish Question" in quite the same way.

In France as well, organized ideological anti-Semitism emerged at the end of the nineteenth century. It, too, as a recent exhaustive study of anti-Semitism at the time of the Dreyfus affair makes clear, was a reaction to the crisis of modernization. [17] Frenchmen disoriented by fundamental changes in society and economy identified Jews as the agents of dislocation, decadence, and decay. Small traders and businessmen, students, the lower clergy, journalists, ex-army officers, members of the liberal professions, peasants, and, above all, bourgeois and petit bourgeois Catholics elected anti-Semitic deputies, joined militant anti-Semitic leagues, bought anti-Semitic newspapers like the Catholic daily *La Croix* and Drumont's daily *La Libre Parole*, boycotted Jewish shops, demonstrated and rioted.

The outpouring of anti-Jewish feeling at the time of the Dreyfus affair was so intense that a few scholars have concluded—wrongly, I believe—that anti-Semitism was stronger there before World War I than in either Germany or Austria.[18] It is easy to understand why they reached this conclusion: Public anti-Semitism in France crystallized around a dramatic series of events in one of Europe's great capitals, whereas in Germany it was far more diffuse, without a similarly spellbinding focal point. In one sense, the eventual vindication of the Dreyfusard position, which came in part with his retrial and pardon in 1899 and in full with his acquittal in 1906, testifies to the weakness of the forces of illiberalism in France, including public anti-Semitism, vis-à-vis the forces supporting the principles of the Revolution. In France, unlike Germany, conservative nationalists did not dominate the organs of the state. On the contrary, the parties of reaction were in rout during the Third Republic, their enemies—the parties of the Left—in the ascendant,[19] while in Germany the only politicians whom Jews could expect to defend their civil equality—the Progressives—were weak, ineffectual, and less than vigorous in their defense of Jewish interests. To be sure, many of the liberals and socialists who eventually rallied around the Dreyfusard standard were not entirely free of anti-Semitism themselves (left-wing, anti-capitalist anti-Semitism was born in France, after all), but when, after some hesitation, they realized that the anti-Semitism of the Right threatened the fundamental principles of republican government, they chose to oppose the anti-Semitic enemies of Dreyfus and the Republic.

The erroneous perception that public anti-Semitism was more powerful in France than in Germany is belied in another way as well by the events of the Dreyfus affair, or, to be more precise, by the social situation out of which it arose. There would have been no Dreyfus affair had Jews not had access to positions of status and honor in French society. Dreyfus was the first Jew to be promoted to the army general staff, although hardly the first to be appointed to the officer corps. Republican institutions in France, however imperfect their actual operation may have been, opened up government and military service to Jews who wished to seek advancement in this way. (In Germany and Austria, of course, state-sanctioned discrimination successfully barred Jews from becoming officers.) Paradoxically, then, the Dreyfus affair may testify less to the failure of emancipation in France than to its success, for in retrospect the forces promoting the integration of Jews into the mainstream of society appear to have been stronger than those working against it.

In Great Britain and the United States the history of anti-Semitism in the nineteenth and early twentieth centuries took a very different course from that on the Continent. In spheres of life outside the purview of the state, discrimination and defamation were at times quite common, particularly in America between 1880 and 1950. In public life, however, anti-Semitism made few significant inroads. The major political parties did not incorporate anti-Semitic planks into their election programs. There were no clamorous campaigns by voluntary organizations to pressure Congress or Parliament to legislate a second-class citizenship for Jews. Neither the British nor the American government condoned the exclusion of Jews from state offices and posts (although undoubtedly discrimination occurred). In general, ideological anti-Semitism played an insignificant role in Anglo-American political life, remaining for the most part on the periphery of the established party system. During the Great Depression, anti-Semitic demagogues like Sir Oswald Mosley, who founded and led the British Union of Fascists from 1932 to 1939, and Father Charles Coughlin, whose radio program reached millions of Americans in the late 1930s, succeeded tem-

1870s on to "the very presence of the unique Jewish community among the other nations."[23] Although he does not deny the causal importance of stresses and strains within the larger societies in which Jews lived, Katz believes that the decisive factor was the failure of the Jewish people to disappear of its own volition as a self-conscious particularistic group. With emancipation, he correctly points out, both friends and foes expected Jews to shed their characteristic rites and symbols and abandon their family exclusivity, occupational imbalance, and mutual solidarity. However, instead of assimilating completely into Gentile society, Jews simultaneously managed to maintain their collective identity while also achieving great prominence in cultural and economic life. This created "a certain uneasiness, not to say a sense of outright scandal."[24] Although Jews' accomplishments outside their own communities tended to weaken traditional Jewish loyalties, anti-Semites did not see the consequences of emancipation in this way. In their view, Jewry was growing more powerful all the time, threatening the material and spiritual welfare of state and society.

Although the failure of the Jewish people to disappear as a collective entity after emancipation may have contributed to the resurgence of anti-Semitism at the end of the last century, it is unlikely that this constituted the decisive cause among those activating anti-Semitism at this time. For if Katz's interpretation were correct, it would follow that in those countries where Jewish solidarity and particularism remained strongest in the post-emancipation era, anti-Semitism would have been at its deadliest. But, in fact, just the opposite was true. In the years 1870–1939, in the liberal states of the West—Great Britain and the United States—where Jewish ethnicity and visibility were not radically attenuated, public anti-Semitism was weaker than it was in Germany, where assimilation had taken a far more extreme course. To be sure, Jews were not merely the passive victims of anti-Semitism, their conduct irrelevant to the history of Jew-hatred. Their occupational patterns, political sympathies, eco-

nomic mobility, and perhaps even manners and morals exacerbated pre-existing prejudices and provided motifs and emphases
for deeply rooted antipathies. But they did not determine the
different paths anti-Semitism took in the various countries of the
West. Only the histories of those states, of the social, political, and
economic contexts in which anti-Semitism developed, can explain why this hatred ended in overwhelming tragedy in some
places and merely psychological discomfort and material depriva-
tion in others.

NOTES

I wish to acknowledge the helpful comments on this essay that I received
from Jack Rakove, James Diehl, and Alvin Rosenfeld.

1. Michael N. Dobkowski, *The Tarnished Dream: The Basis of American
Anti-Semitism* (Westport, Conn., 1979); Colin Holmes, *Anti-Semitism in British Society, 1876–1939* (New York, 1979).

2. For example, see Shmuel Ettinger's comments on the contrast
between "early anti-Jewishness" and "modern anti-Semitism" in *A History
of the Jewish People,* ed. Haim Hillel Ben-Sasson (Cambridge, Mass., 1976),
p. 871.

3. George L. Mosse, *Toward the Final Solution: A History of European
Racism* (New York, 1978), p. xvi.

4. Leon Poliakov, *The Aryan Myth: A History of Racist and Nationalist Ideas
in Europe,* trans. Edmund Howard (New York, 1977).

5. Jacob Katz, *From Prejudice to Destruction: Anti-Semitism, 1700–1933*
(Cambridge, Mass., 1980), pp. 56–57.

6. Johann Gottlieb Fichte, *Beitrag zur Berichtigung der Urteile des Pub-
likums über die französische Revolution* (Jena, 1793), p. 101, quoted in J. Katz,
From Prejudice to Destruction, p. 57.

7. Yosef Haim Yerushalmi, *Assimilation and Racial Anti-Semitism: The
Iberian and the German Models,* Leo Baeck Memorial Lecture 26 (New York,
1982), pp. 14–16.

8. Ibid., p. 22.

9. Ernest L. Freud, ed., *The Letters of Sigmund Freud and Arnold Zweig,*
trans. Elaine and William Robson-Scott (New York, 1970), p. 3.

10. The most recent survey of modern anti-Semitism, Jacob Katz's
From Prejudice to Destruction, focuses almost exclusively on the intellectual
history of anti-Semitism and consequently fails to ask why certain ideas
found widespread acceptance in some countries and not others. See my

review of this work in the *Association for Jewish Studies Newsletter*, no. 22 (Summer 1982), pp. 11–12, 16; Katz's response, "Misreadings of Anti-Semitism," *Commentary* 76, no. 1 (July 1983): 39–44; and the exchange of letters between Katz and myself, *Commentary* 76, no. 6 (Dec. 1983): 30, 32–33.

11. For a discussion of the inadequacy of survey analysis as a tool for studying anti-Semitism, from a perspective different from my own, see Lucy S. Dawidowicz, "Can Anti-Semitism be Measured?" in her collection, *The Jewish Presence: Essays on Identity and History* (New York, 1977), pp. 193–215.

12. Quoted in Harry Stone, "Dickens and the Jews," *Victorian Studies* 2 (1959): 223.

13. Shulamit Volkov, *The Rise of Popular Antimodernism in Germany: The Urban Master Artisans, 1873–1896* (Princeton, 1978), p. 317.

14. Quoted in Peter G. J. Pulzer, *The Rise of Political Anti-Semitism in Germany and Austria* (New York, 1964), p. 119.

15. Fritz Stern's remarks on illiberalism in modern German political culture are germane: "The amazing quality of German illiberalism was its pervasiveness. The political system may have formally imposed it, the class antagonisms may have sharpened it, the revered army may have embodied it, the schools and universities may have taught it, but it had evolved for a long time and was part of a cultural style. At every juncture in his career, a German would learn illiberal attitudes or see illiberal models in positions of authority: there were few, if any, accepted models of playfulness or tolerant dissent." *The Failure of Illiberalism: Essays on the Political Culture of Modern Germany* (New York, 1972), p. xviii.

16. Peter Gay, *Freud, Jews and Other Germans: Masters and Victims in Modernist Culture* (New York, 1978), p. 19.

17. Stephen Wilson, *Ideology and Experience: Antisemitism in France at the Time of the Dreyfus Affair* (Rutherford, N.J., 1982).

18. For example, Hannah Arendt, *Antisemitism,* part 1 of *The Origins of Totalitarianism* (New York, 1968), p. 79; and Peter Pulzer, "Why Was There a Jewish Question in Imperial Germany?" *Leo Baeck Institute Year Book* 25 (1980): 133.

19. Michael Marrus and Robert Paxton, in describing the historical background to Vichy policy toward the Jews, caution against exaggerating the scope of *fin de siècle* anti-Semitism in France, despite its exuberance. "The Dreyfusards won, after all, in the end. Electoral nationalism collapsed after its apogee in 1902, and its energies fragmented . . . even *La Croix* could step back from the brink, and seemed to be moderating at the end." *Vichy France and the Jews* (New York, 1981), p. 31. In their introduction they point out that although France had been the first European state to extend full rights to Jews, Frenchmen were also among the ideological pioneers of secular anti-Semitism in the century following emancipation. Both tradi-

tions existed side by side, jostling each other for dominance. "During the Third Republic, the tolerant tradition prevailed, almost to the end, against the xenophobic one" (pp. xiii–xiv).

20. For example, see the account of the Murphy riots of the late 1860s in Walter L. Arnstein, *Protestant versus Catholic in Mid-Victorian England: Mr. Newdegate and the Nuns* (Columbia, Missouri, 1982), ch. 7.

21. Ismar Schorsch, *Jewish Reactions to German Anti-Semitism, 1870–1914* (New York, 1972), pp. 47–48.

22. Paula Hyman, *From Dreyfus to Vichy: The Remaking of French Jewry, 1906–1939* (New York, 1979), pp. 118–119.

23. Katz, *From Prejudice to Destruction*, p. 322.

24. Katz, "Misreadings of Anti-Semitism," p. 43.

Todd M. Endelman

American Anti-Semitism

Jonathan D. Sarna

The fact that a volume on the history of anti-Semitism includes a brief American perspective is itself noteworthy. Earlier surveys of anti-Semitism, whether found in the *American Jewish Year Book* or in as scholarly a volume as Koppel Pinson's *Essays on Antisemitism* (1946), studiously avoided including any mention of America in the context of worldwide Judeophobia. To speak of American anti-Semitism and European anti-Semitism in the same breath seemed almost blasphemous. Even to speak of American anti-Semitism on its own took courage. As late as 1947, a scholarly article dealing with anti-Semitism that appeared in the *Publications of the American Jewish Historical Society* began with an elaborate justification. "We can," it explained, "no longer dismiss anti-Semitism with a wave of the hand or a flourish of the pen. As an influence in American Jewish life—although a negative one to be sure—its study comes within the scope of this Society's activities." [1]

Today nobody would think that undertaking a study of American anti-Semitism requires advance justification. Not only has the subject acquired legitimacy, but also it has now become one of the most intensely examined aspects of American life, the subject of innumerable books and monographs, [2] and the focus of full sessions at the annual meetings of such prestigious scholarly associations as the American Historical Association and the Organization of American Historians. No consensus has emerged from all of these vigorous efforts, not even a clear definition of what anti-Semitism in the American context means. But two questions do seem to me to have emerged as central:

1. How important a role has anti-Semitism played in American life?

2. Is America different in terms of anti-Semitism, and if so, how?

The Role of Anti-Semitism

With regard to the first question, the significance of anti-Semitism in American life, there are, as might be expected, several divergent opinions. The most traditional one, which I label minimalist, considers anti-Semitism to be a late and alien phenomenon on the American scene: a post–Civil War development, linked to the rise of both "scientific" racism and anti-immigrant nativism, and then confined largely to the ranks of the disaffected. Earlier on in America, according to this view, such Judeophobic attitudes failed to take root. Jews were instead considered, as Oscar Handlin put it, "wonderful in their past achievements . . . still more wonderful in their preservation."[3] Isolated incidents did occur—Peter Stuyvesant's effort to keep Jews out of New Amsterdam, the recall of Consul Mordecai Noah from Tunis on account of his religion, or General Grant's Order #11 ousting Jews from his war zone—but in the minimalist interpretation these serve only as exceptions that prove the rule. Since in every case the severity of the evil decree was somehow mitigated and Jews ultimately emerged triumphant, these incidents are not viewed as "incompatible with the total acceptance of Jews as Americans."[4] Minimalists imply that hate would cease if Americans would only return to the virtuous ways of their forebears.

As against this view, there is another and diametrically opposite perspective on anti-Semitism in America, which I label
maximalist. Maximalists, influenced by recent trends in American
historiography, particularly the study of racism, find anti-Semites
stalking the length and breadth of American history, from colonial times down to the present. They know, as minimalists do not,
that anti-Jewish slurs, discrimination against Jews, even acts of
violence directed against Jewish institutions have stained the
pages of American history for over three centuries. Blood libels,
professional anti-Semitic crusaders, and avowed Nazis have, at
one time or another, also appeared on the American scene. The
conclusion that maximalists draw from this is plainly stated by
Michael Selzer in his *"Kike!": A Documentary History of Anti-Semitism
in America:*

> There is no reason to believe that from the vast reservoir of
> bigotry, and specifically of anti-Semitism, that exists in this
> country, a new wave of Jew-baiting, perhaps even of persecu-
> tion and murder, may not arise.[5]

"It"—meaning the Holocaust—"could have happened here,"
maximalists often contend, and they darkly warn that "it" may
happen yet.

Inevitably, a third view lies between these two polar extremes, and that is the middle ground or centrist position. Centrists have no quarrel with those who find manifestations of anti-
Semitism throughout American history: The facts speak for
themselves. Every kind of prejudice found in Europe can be found
in America, *if* one searches hard enough. Centrists point out,
however, that Jews have also enjoyed thoroughly harmonious
relations with non-Jews throughout American Jewish history,
and that ideological philo-Semitism forms at least as much a part
of America's cultural heritage as its opposite. Anti-Semitism,
centrists insist, must be seen in its proper historical perspective. It

is only one aspect of a larger and more complex dynamic that forms the true picture of Jewish-Gentile relations in the United States.

The Centrist Perspective

No full-scale history of American anti-Semitism written from a centrist perspective yet exists. In outline form, however, such a history can readily be sketched out.

Beginning in the colonial period, Jews faced rejection, prejudice, and even occasional violence in America, while anti-Jewish literary stereotypes abounded. "'Jew' was still a dirty word," Jacob R. Marcus writes, "and it was hardly rare to see the Jews denigrated as such in the press."[6] As early as the mid-seventeenth century a New Amsterdam Jew named David Ferera, found guilty of insulting a bailiff, received an inordinately strict punishment on account of his religion. During the period of English rule, New York Jews suffered a violent mob attack against one of their funeral corteges and quite a few desecrations of their cemeteries, besides more regular cases of discrimination and defamation. Yet Jews also prospered in colonial America and maintained close, sometimes even intimate relations with their non-Jewish neighbors. After weighing the evidence as a whole, Marcus concludes that Jews found more acceptance in America "than in any other land in the world."[7] The hostility of some colonial settlers toward Jews, he implies, cannot be ignored but must not be exaggerated.

After independence, the Jewish situation improved, but not so much as some would believe. Although non-Protestants received political rights, the baiting of Jews became an accepted part of political mud-slinging, even when—as in the case of John Israel of Pittsburgh—the candidate in question may not have been Jewish at all. Various recent monographs demonstrate that the range of anti-Semitic incidents in the young republic spanned the spectrum from literary and cultural stereotyping, social and economic discrimination, attacks on Jewish property, all the way to blood libels and lurid descriptions of purported anti-Christian sentiments in classical Jewish texts. In 1820, New York's *German Correspondent* admitted:

> The Jews are not generally regarded with a favorable eye; and "Jew" is an epithet which is frequently uttered in a tone bordering on contempt. Say what you will, prejudices against the Jews exist here, and subject them to inconveniences from which other citizens of the United States are exempt.[8]

James Gordon Bennett's widely read *New York Herald* displayed particular vehemence in its denunciation of Jews. Although Bennett enjoyed lambasting a host of targets and was quite capable of printing philo-Semitic articles as well, his most inflammatory rhetoric evoked the darkest days of medieval disputations:

> Here are pictured forth, from their own sacred writings, the Talmud, which is considered a second part of the Bible, the real opinion of the Jews on the original and Sacred Founder of Christianity. . . . In the midst of Christians, surrounded by Christian usages, the Jews may conceal these terrible opinions and doctrines—may attempt to beguile and deceive those among whom they live, in order the better to crush all religion under the secret poison of infidelity and atheism, but their Talmuds and Targums are evidences against them.[9]

Similarly medieval were characterizations of Jews in early American literature. Louis Harap, in his comprehensive book *The Image of the Jew in American Literature* (1974), finds "invidious stereotypes of the pawnbroker and businessman," along with such timeless motifs as the "Jew's daughter," the Jewish hunchback, and the Jewish criminal in popular ante-bellum fiction. George Lippard's best-selling *The Quaker City or The Monks of Monk Hall* (1844) portrayed a hump-backed Jewish forger, Gabriel Van Gelt, who swindles, blackmails, and commits murder for the sake of money. Joseph Holt Ingraham's tales, best-sellers too, offered a whole cast of dark-eyed Shylocks, beautiful Jewish daughters, and revolting Jewish criminals. But it must be emphasized that Jews rarely appear as lone villains in early American literature. Not only do they have Gentile accomplices, but also in many cases they give expression to a wise and sympathetic understanding of Jewish-Gentile relations ("Te Christian plead humbly to te Jew ven he would have money, and curses him ven he no more needs him"), and of history too ("Under the despotic governments of the old world [the Jew's] political and personal rights have been the football of tyranny and cupidity"). Harap's summary seems apt:

> Novels reveal attitudes and not necessarily behavior . . . probably actual relations were less acerbic than those reflected in [literature]. However, the reality must have been ambivalent at best.[10]

Ambivalence is the appropriate word. Conflicting emotions, changing experiences, and divergent influences pulled people now one way, now the other. At times the lure of the exotic opened doors to Jews. Rural Americans traveled miles just to catch a glimpse of one of God's chosen people. Joseph Jonas of Cincinnati, for example, recalled:

> Many persons of the Nazarene faith residing from 50 to 100 miles from the city, hearing there were Jews living in Cincinnati, came into town for the special purpose of viewing and conversing with some of "the children of Israel, the holy people of God," as they termed us.[11]

As was true in the case of Asian immigrants, however, the lure of the exotic frequently gave way to fear of the unknown. Outsiders came to view Jews as an alien force, a people apart, "deficient," as Charles King (at one time the president of Columbia College) wrote in 1823, "in that single national attachment which binds the man to the soil of his nativity, and makes him the

Jonathan D. Sarna

exclusive patriot of his own country." [12] As patronizing curiosity gave way to xenophobic delusion, doors closed and Jews were kept out.

A second, even more powerful source of ambivalence was the pervasive tension between the "mythical Jew," that cursed figure of Christian tradition deeply embedded in Western culture, and the "Jew next door," who seemingly gave the lie to every element of the stereotype. [13] Usually, it was the mythical Jew—the unscrupulous moneylender, the eternal wanderer, the satanic Christ-killer—who was flayed by anti-Semites. If they sometimes realized that Jews of their acquaintance did not fit the mold, the mold was often too deeply ingrained to change; it was easier to live with the contradiction. "Them Jews—I don't mean you," is a phrase one upstate New Yorker still remembers having heard from her neighbors. Thomas Jefferson, in spite of having several Jewish acquaintances, continued to think Jews morally depraved. Henry Ford actually believed that all the "good Jews" of the country, including his friend Rabbi Leo Franklin, would rally to his crusade against the "international Jew." [14]

"When a delusion cannot be dissipated by the facts of reality, it probably does not spring from reality," Freud wrote. [15] Dissonance between received wisdom and perceived wisdom was particularly strong in the case of Jews. From colonial days onward, Jews and Christians cooperated with one another, maintaining close social and economic relations. Intermarriage rates, a reliable if unwelcome sign of religious harmony, periodically rose to high levels. And individual Jews thrived, often rising to positions of wealth and power. Yet popular prejudice based on received wisdom continued nonetheless. Even some slight manifestation of a "typical Jewish trait" brought all the old charges back to the fore.

Ambivalence is a theme that emerges clearly during the Civil War. According to Bertram Korn, "anti-Jewish prejudice was actually a characteristic expression of the [Civil War] age, part and parcel of the economic and social upheaval effectuated by the war." Korn adduced evidence of anti-Jewish writings and activities both in the North and South; "the Jews were a . . . popular scapegoat in all areas."[16] Far from being an isolated exception, General Grant's expulsion order was part of a larger pattern. Yet at the same time Jews rose in the ranks of both armies; rabbis won the right to serve as chaplains; Judah Benjamin became a key Confederate leader; and President Lincoln showed unprecedented concern for Jews' civil liberties. In the Civil War as earlier, Jews in general suffered because of what the word "Jew" symbolized, while individual Jews won the respect of their fellow citizens and emerged from the fratricidal struggle more self-assured than they had ever been before.

In the post–Civil War era, during Reconstruction and in the Gilded Age, many "Israelites"—as some called themselves to distinguish real Jews from mythical ones—prospered with the American business boom. Gaudy showpiece temples, the Jewish form of conspicuous consumption, testified to the community's new status and wealth. Jews entered the upper class. The upper class, however, had at best mixed feelings about whether to welcome Jewish parvenus. In the words of the Boston *Saturday Evening Gazette,* quoted by John Higham, "It is strange that a nation that boasts so many good traits should be so obnoxious."[17] Ultimately, some individual Jews won acceptance, while Jews as a group continued to meet with considerable hostility. Long before Joseph Seligman made his trip to Saratoga and was turned away, complaints about discrimination and prejudice filled the pages of Jewish newspapers.

By all accounts, anti-Semitism crested in America during the half-century preceding World War II. During this era of nativism and then isolationism, Jews faced physical attacks, many forms of discrimination, and intense vilification in print, on the airwaves, in movies, and on stage. A series of highly publicized anti-Semitic episodes took place: the lynching of Leo Frank, the ravings of Henry Ford, the blood libel in Massena, New York, and anti-Jewish speeches by notables too numerous to list.[18] Yet the same period witnessed the growth of the interfaith movement, a great increase in the number of Jews on college campuses and in government service, and unprecedented cooperation between Jews and non-Jews in areas of social service. Once again, the historical picture is a mixed one, anti-Semitism forming only part of a larger story.

Professor Endelman has pointed to the theme of anti-modernism as a possible explanation for post-Emancipation forms of anti-Semitism. I think that this approach to anti-Semitism, viewing it as a cultural code, offers rich potential.[19] As I read the paroxysms of America's Jew-haters, I am repeatedly struck by how frequently Jews receive blame for whatever happens to be wrong with modern society, from music to the movies to the New Deal. Jews can be condemned as capitalists and lambasted as communists in the same manifestos. Yet I fear that explaining anti-Semitism through anti-modernism is to forget that anti-Semitism is a *form* of anti-modernism. By changing the term we are not freed from the obligation to explain *why* anti-modernism comes and goes. Anti-modernism adds to our understanding by broadening our sphere of vision and stimulating new avenues of exploration. But it leaves the complex question of causality still unanswered.

Is American Anti-Semitism Different?

I now turn to the second question posed at the beginning: Is America different in terms of anti-Semitism, and if so, how? Such questions, demanding exhaustive research in comparative history, might with greater prudence be left unanswered. Nevertheless, I want to suggest five factors which, when taken together, do seem to me to lend a special color to American anti-Semitism, differentiating its history from the history of anti-Semitism elsewhere in the Diaspora. I realize, of course, that countries are subject to change. Furthermore, by saying that America is different, I am not by any means implying that it is altogether different, but only in several—critical—respects.

1. In America, Jews have always fought anti-Semites freely. Never having received their emancipation as an "award," they have had no fears of losing it. Instead, from the beginning they made full use of their rights to freedom of speech. As early as 1784, a "Jew Broker"—probably Haym Salomon—responded publicly and forcefully to the anti-Semitic charges of a prominent Quaker lawyer, not hesitating to remind him that his "own religious sectary" could also form "very proper subjects of criticism and animadversion."[20] A few years later, Christian missionaries and their supporters faced Jewish polemics no less strident in tone. Where European Jews prided themselves on their "forebearance" in the face of attack, Rabbi Isaac Mayer Wise boasted that he was a "malicious, biting, pugnacious, challenging, and mocking monster of the pen."[21] Louis Marshall and Stephen Wise, early twentieth-century spokesmen of American Jewry, may have been more civil, but as readers of their voluminous letters know, they were no less bold. In defense of Jewish rights, they did battle even with the President of the United States.

2. American anti-Semitism has always had to compete with other forms of animus. Racism, anti-Quakerism, Anglophobia, anti-Catholicism, anti-Masonry, anti-Mormonism, anti-Orientalism, nativism, anti-Teutonism, anti-Communism—these and other waves have periodically swept over the American landscape, scarring and battering citizens. Because the objects are so varied, hatred is diffused and no group experiences for long the full brunt of national odium. Furthermore, most Americans retain bitter memories of days past when they or their ancestors were the objects of malevolence. The American strain of anti-Semitism is thus less potent than its European counterpart, and it faces a larger number of natural competitors. To reach epidemic proportions, it must first crowd out a vast number of contending hatreds.

3. Anti-Semitism is more foreign to American ideals than to

Jonathan D. Sarna

European ones. The central documents of the Republic assure Jews of liberty; its first president conferred upon them his blessing. The fact that anti-Semitism can properly be branded "un-American," although no protection in the formal sense—the nation has betrayed its ideals innumerable times—grants Jews a measure of protection not found in Europe. There anti-Semites could always claim a legitimacy stemming from times past when the *Volk* ruled and Jews knew their place. American romantics could point to nothing even remotely similar in their own past. The Founding Fathers, whatever they personally thought of Jews, gave them full equality. "Who are you, or what are you . . . that in a *free* country you dare to trample on any sectary whatever of people?" Haym Salomon had demanded back in 1784. Half a century later, Isaac Leeser charged that it was "contrary to the spirit of the Constitution of the country for the many to combine to do the smallest minority the injury of depriving them of their conscientious conviction by systematic efforts."[22] Non-Jews could respond by pointing to America's supposedly "Christian character"—a view of American society occasionally recognized by no less august a body than the Supreme Court. Nevertheless, the Constitution has proved to be a potent weapon in the Jews' defense. German Jews could appeal to no similar document.

4. America's religious tradition—what has been called "the great tradition of the American churches"—is inhospitable to anti-Semitism. Religious freedom and diversity, Church-state separation, denominationalism, and voluntarism, the key components of this tradition as described by Winthrop Hudson and Sydney Ahlstrom,[23] militate against the kind of "Deutschtum-Judentum" dichotomy that existed in Germany. In America, where religious pluralism rules supreme, there is no national church from which Jews stand apart. People speak instead of American Protestants, American Catholics, and American Jews, implying, at least as an ideal, that all three stand equal in importance.

5. American politics resists anti-Semitism. In a two-party

system where close elections are the rule, neither party can long afford to alienate any major bloc of voters. The politics of hatred have thus largely been confined to noisy third parties and single-issue fringe groups. When anti-Semitism is introduced into the political arena—as it has been periodically since the days of the Federalists—major candidates generally repudiate it. America's most successful politicians build broad-based coalitions, highly nebulous in their ideology. They seek support from respectable elements all across the political spectrum. Experience has taught them that appeals to national unity win more elections than appeals to narrow provincialism or to bigotry.

Of course, the fact that America has been "exceptional" in relation to Jews should not obscure the sad reality that there has always been anti-Semitism in America, and that it still continues to exist. Complacency is a luxury that Jews cannot afford—anywhere. But if America has not been heaven for Jews (and as we have seen it hasn't been), it has been as far from hell as any Diaspora Jewish community. History, as I read it, gives American Jews cause neither for undue celebration nor for undue alarm. Instead, it records both the manifold blessings that America has bestowed upon Jews, and, simultaneously, the need for Jews, even in America, to remain eternally vigilant.

NOTES

Portions of this essay first appeared in somewhat different form in *Commentary*. I am grateful to the editors of *Commentary* for permitting me to republish them here.

1. Leonard A. Greenberg, "Some American Anti-Semitic Publications of the Late 19th Century," *Publications of the American Jewish Historical Society* 37 (1947): 421.
2. A recent research guide lists 219 items dealing with America alone; see Robert Singerman, *Antisemitic Propaganda: An Annotated Bibliography and Research Guide* (New York, 1982), pp. 355–376. An earlier guide, Melvin M.

Tumin's *An Inventory and Appraisal of Research on American Anti-Semitism* (New York, 1961), remains valuable.

3. Oscar Handlin, *Adventure in Freedom* (New York, 1954), p. 175.

4. Ibid., p. 183.

5. Michael Selzer, *"Kike!"*: *A Documentary History of Anti-Semitism in America* (New York, 1972), p. 6; see also Ernest Volkman, *A Legacy of Hate: Anti-Semitism in America* (New York, 1982).

6. Jacob R. Marcus, *The Colonial American Jew*, vol. 3 (Detroit, 1970), p. 1335; cf. 1113–1134.

7. Ibid., p. 1336.

8. *The German Correspondent* 1 (1820): 6.

9. *New York Herald*, November 18, 1837; see Jonathan D. Sarna, *Jacksonian Jew: The Two Worlds of Mordecai Noah* (New York, 1981), pp. 119–25.

10. Louis Harap, *The Image of the Jew in American Literature* (Philadelphia, 1974), p. 71, and see pp. 46–81. See also Louise A. Mayo, "The Ambivalent Image: The Perception of the Jew in Nineteenth-Century America" (Ph.D. diss., C.U.N.Y., 1977), and Michael Dobkowski, *The Tarnished Dream* (Westport, Conn., 1979).

11. Morris U. Schappes, ed., *A Documentary History of the Jews in the United States, 1654–1875* (New York, 1971), p. 226.

12. *A Letter to Charles King From an American Jew* (New York, 1823), pp. 3–4; Sarna, *Jacksonian Jew*, pp. 179–180.

13. Jonathan D. Sarna, "The 'Mythical Jew' and the 'Jew Next Door' in Nineteenth-Century America," in David Gerber, ed., *Anti-Semitism in American History* (Urbana, Ill., 1986), pp. 57–78.

14. Robert H. Ruxin, "The Jewish Farmer and the Small-Town Jewish Community: Schoharie County, New York," *American Jewish Archives* 29 (Apr. 1977): 13; Andrew A. Lipscomb, ed., *The Writings of Thomas Jefferson* (Washington, 1904), vol. 10, p. 382; Lester J. Cappon, ed., *The Adams-Jefferson Letters*, vol. 2 (Chapel Hill, 1959), p. 383; Keith Sward, *The Legend of Henry Ford* (New York, 1972), p. 147.

15. Sigmund Freud, *A General Introduction to Psychoanalysis* (New York, 1953), p. 262.

16. Bertram W. Korn, *American Jewry and the Civil War* (New York, 1970), pp. 156, 187.

17. John Higham, *Send These to Me* (New York, 1975), p. 124.

18. Nathan C. Belth, *A Promise to Keep: A Narrative of the American Encounter with Anti-Semitism* (New York, 1979), surveys the field.

19. See Jackson Lears, *No Place of Grace: Antimodernism and the Transformation of American Culture 1880–1920* (New York, 1981).

20. Jacob R. Marcus, *American Jewry Documents: Eighteenth Century* (Cincinnati, 1959), pp. 41–46.

21. Jonathan D. Sarna, "The American Jewish Response to Nine-teenth-Century Christian Missions," *The Journal of American History* 68 (June 1981): 47.

22. Marcus, *American Jewry Documents,* p. 43; Sarna, "American Jewish Response," p. 46.

23. Winthrop Hudson, *The Great Tradition of the American Churches* (New York, 1963); Sydney E. Ahlstrom, *A Religious History of the American People* (New Haven, 1972), pp. 379–384.

Contributors

DAVID BERGER is Professor of History at Brooklyn College and the Graduate School of the City University of New York. He is the author of *The Jewish-Christian Debate in the High Middle Ages*, which was awarded the Medieval Academy of America's John Nicholas Brown Prize for 1983, and of numerous articles on Jewish-Christian relations and the intellectual history of the Jews. He is co-author (with Michael Wyschogrod) of *Jews and "Jewish Christianity"*, and editor of *The Legacy of Jewish Migration: 1881 and Its Impact*.

ROBERT CHAZAN is Professor of History at Queens College and at the Graduate School of the City University of New York, where he also serves as the Director of the Center for Jewish Studies. He is the author of *Medieval Jewry in Northern France; Church, State and Jew in the Middle Ages;* and *European Jewry and the First Crusade* (forthcoming).

JEREMY COHEN holds the Samuel and Esther Melton Chair of Jewish History and Jewish Studies at the Ohio State University. His publications include *The Friars and the Jews: The Evolution of Medieval Anti-Judaism*, which was the 1983 recipient of the National Jewish Book Award for Scholarship.

SHAYE J. D. COHEN is Professor of Jewish History at the Jewish Theological Seminary of America. He is the author of *Josephus in Galilee and Rome: His Vita and Development as a Historian, From the Maccabees to the Mishnah: A Profile of Judaism* (forthcoming), and numerous scholarly articles on ancient Jewish history.

TODD M. ENDELMAN is Professor of History at the University of Michigan. He is the author of *The Jews of Georgian England, 1714–1830: Tradition and Change in a Liberal Society,* which won the National Jewish Book Award for History and the A. S. Diamond Prize of the Jewish Historical Society of England. His research and writing focus on the history of the Jews in England and the social history of the European and American Jewish communities in the modern period.

LOUIS H. FELDMAN is Professor of Classics at Yeshiva University. He has received fellowships from the Guggenheim Foundation and the American Council of Learned Societies, among others. He is the translator and editor of Books 18 through 20 of Josephus's Jewish *Antiquities* for the Loeb Classical Library. His *Josephus and Modern Scholarship* received the Judaica Reference Book Award from the Association of Jewish Libraries in 1985.

JANE S. GERBER is Director, Institute for Sephardic Studies and Associate Professor of Jewish History at the Graduate Center of the City University of New York. She served as President of the Association for Jewish Studies from 1980 to 1983 and is book review editor of *Jewish Social Studies.* She is the author of *Jewish Society in Fez* and editor of the forthcoming volumes *Case Studies in the Jewish Political Tradition* and *Jewish Peoples: Ethnographic Studies.*

JONATHAN D. SARNA is Associate Professor of American Jewish History at Hebrew Union College–Jewish Institute of Religion, and Academic Director of its Center for the Study of the American Jewish Experience. He is the author of *Jacksonian Jew: The Two Worlds of Mordecai Noah, People Walk on Their Heads: Moses Weinberger's Jews and Judaism in New York,* and *The American Jewish Experience: A Reader.*

Index

Egypt, expulsion of Jews from, 31
Emancipation, of Jews, 9–11
England, anti-Semitism in,
    108–109
Epictetus, 35
Epistle to Yemen (Maimonides),
    90
Euphrates (philosopher), 31

Feisal (king), 88
Felix, 26
Feudal society, Jews in, 51, 59,
    60–61, 64–65 n.
Fichte, Johann, 98
Flaccus, 22–24, 34
Ford, Henry, 121
France, anti-Semitism in, 106–
    107, 110
French Revolution, 9
Freud, Sigmund, 100, 121

Germany, anti-Semitism in, in
        Middle Ages, 55–56
    in modern world, 97–98,
        101–102, 105–108, 110
Government, maturation of, in
        Middle Ages, 58–59
    protection of Jews by, 6, 21. See
        also *Ruling class.*
Governmental anti-Semitism, 16–
    21
Grant, Ulysses S., 122
Great Britain, anti-Semitism in,
    108–109
*Greek and Latin Authors on Jews and
        Judaism,* 29, 30, 37 n., 40–
        41 n., 45

Ḥadith, 76, 78–79, 88
Hadrian, 45–47
Haman, 16
Harap, Louis, 119–120
Ḥatti Ḥumayun, 86
Hecataeus, 17, 30, 33
Herodotus, 32
Historian, objectives of, 3–4
Horace, 33–34

Iberian anti-Semitism, in Middle
        Ages, 8, 68
    in modern world, 98
Idumaeans, 33–34
*Image of the Jew in American Litera-
        ture, The,* 119
Ingraham, Joseph Holt, 120
Interfaith movement, in America,
        growth of, 123
Islam. See also *Muslims.*
    anti-Semitism and, **73–93**
    modern, impact of West on, 87
    relationship of, with Judaism,
        13
        four main periods of,
            75–76
    role of Abraham in, 79
    role of Christians in, 86

Jacob b. Yekutiel, 55
Jefferson, Thomas, 121
Jerusalem, destruction of, in 70
    C.E., 45
Jew(s). See also *Judaism.*
    accusations against, 29–36, 44,
        53, 57–58, 62–63, 68–70,
        95–96, 110

Jew(s) (*continued*)
  alliance of, with ruling class, 21,
    25–26, 36–37, 57
  as aliens, 6–13 passim, 56–57,
    99, 110, 120–121
  Ashkenazic, in Middle Ages,
    49–65
  association of, with modernity,
    11, 105, 109
  business and, in Middle Ages,
    57–60
  Caesar and, 19
  conversion of, in Spain, 8
  dhimma status of, in Muslim
    world, 80–84
  dietary laws of, 31, 41 n.
  dress regulations for, by Mus-
    lims, 80–81
  emancipation of, 9–11
  expulsion of, from Egypt,
    31
    from Rome, 19–20
  in Christian theology, 5, 53,
    68–69, 71
  in feudal society, 51, 59, 60–61,
    64–65 n.
  portrayal of, in literature, 15,
    29, 103, 119–120
    in media, 88, 107–109,
    118–119, 122
  protection of, by clergy, 6–7
    by government, 6, 21. See
    also *Ruling class.*
  rebellion of, against Rome,
    20–21, 24–25, 27–28, 45
  stereotypes of, 50, 57–58, 61,
    102–103, 118–119, 121
John Chrysostom, 69
Jonas, Joseph, 120
Josephus, 17, 25–26, 30, 32, 34,
  36
Journalism. See *Media* and *Newspapers.*
Judah Maccabee, 18

Judaism. See also *Jew(s).*
  as negating Christian theology,
    53, 71
  confrontation of, with Stoicism,
    35
  relationship of, with Islam, 13
  Reform, 10
  spread of, during reign of Au-
    gustus, 18
Juvenal, 32–33

Katz, Jacob, 110–111, 112–113 n.
*"Kike!": A Documentary History of
  Anti-Semitism,* 117
King, Charles, 120–121
Koran, 76–81
Korn, Bertram, 121–122

Lane, Edward W., 85
Lincoln, Abraham, 122
Lippard, George, 119
Literature, American, 119–120
  English, 103
  Hellenistic-Roman, 15, 29
Lukuas-Andreas, 27
Lysimachus, 31, 33

Maccabee, Judah, 18
Maimonides, 90
*Manners and Customs of the Modern
  Egyptians,* 85
Marcus, Jacob R., 118
Marcus, Ralph, 22
Marranism, 8, 11, 68
Martial, 33
Mecca, 77
Media, portrayal of Jews in, 88,
  107–109, 118–119, 122